Music's CULT ARTISTS

This edition published in 2020 by Dog 'n' Bone Books
An imprint of Ryland Peters & Small Ltd
20–21 Jockey's Fields   341 E 116th St
London WC1R 4BW   New York, NY 10029

www.rylandpeters.com

10 9 8 7 6 5 4 3 2 1

First published in 2016 as *Sound and Vision*.

Text and illustration © John Riordan 2016, 2020
Design © Dog 'n' Bone Books 2016, 2020

A CIP catalog record for this book is available from the Library of Congress
and the British Library.

ISBN: 978 1 912983 28 5

Printed in China

Illustrator: John Riordan
Editor: Caroline West
Designer: Eoghan O'Brien

Commissioning editor: Pete Jorgensen
Art director: Sally Powell
Production manager: Gordana Simakovic
Publishing manager: Penny Craig
Publisher: Cindy Richards

Credit:
"Herman Loves Pauline" by Super Furry Animals (see page 105)
Words and music by Huw Bunford, Cian Ciaran, Dafydd Ieuan,
Guto Pryce, and Gruff Rhys.
Lyrics used by kind permission of Nettwerk Music Group.

MUSIC'S CULT ARTISTS

100 ARTISTS FROM PUNK, ALTERNATIVE, AND INDIE THROUGH TO HIP-HOP, DANCE MUSIC, AND BEYOND

JOHN RIORDAN

DOG 'N' BONE

CONTENTS

INTRODUCTION

I grew up in a musical household. My dad was obsessed with jazz and classical music, and he and my mum played in various groups, orchestras, and choirs, while my brother and I learned piano, trumpet, and oboe. But none of it was my music. Jazz sounded like cold toast and I didn't like the way they sang in opera. Anyway, classical music was boring. I used to fall asleep during the concerts my dad played in (sorry, Dad).* My friends grew up in houses where pop radio was their daily soundtrack (as jazz and classical radio were in mine), but I was only peripherally aware of 1980s pop.

Then, when I was 13, pop music bit me, in the form of early '90s indie bands whose best songs were handpicked for me by discerning friends and recorded on to C90 cassettes. This was in the years before UK indie was shoehorned into the more presentable shape of Britpop. My new musical heroes were young, spiky, and peculiar, with niche appeal. It seemed supremely improbable that the likes of Senseless Things, The Frank and Walters, or Kingmaker would ever trouble the charts. I was already obsessed with comic books and I had finally found their musical equivalent—short, condensed bursts of irreverent pop culture. Soon I had my own CD player and I was going to gigs with friends, staying for the encore, then running for the last train home (with us frequently phoning our parents for a lift when we missed it). My dad seemed pleased that I had found my own music and was quietly encouraging (apart from when he had to pick us up from the station).

Discovering these bands was like opening a small door into a vast and colorful world. In those pre-Internet days, the UK music press was still in decent health, and weekly and monthly rags such as the *NME*, *Melody Maker*, and *Select* became my entertaining and irascible guide to this world. The best of these bands had great characters, with gobby singers making as much noise as they could in the pre-Britpop musical pond. They had backstories and told tales of hedonistic and creative excess that made me want to learn the guitar and start a band. I pored over their interviews, seeking clues to more good music and following up references to other bands, both past and present. I listened to evening shows on BBC Radio 1, in which John Peel and Mark and Lard mixed new releases and session recordings with vintage tracks. I bought new music by Suede, Blur (see page 78), and Oasis (see page 86), as well as albums by The Smiths (see page 46) from ten years previously, and I borrowed Beatles' LPs from my friends' parents. Pop music became an ever-expanding landscape, opening up both the past and future as my tastes broadened. It never stopped expanding.

What you hold in your hands is a result of 20-plus years of musical geekery. There have been times when I've been less active in keeping up with the new stuff or less obsessive in following up the old stuff, but all the while indie/alternative pop music has soundtracked my life.

A word on definitions: as soon as you start trying to define "cult," "alternative," or "indie," these terms break down. "Indie" originally meant that the music was released by an independent record company, but most of the genuinely "indie" labels got bought up by majors, and the term soon morphed into a description of the music itself. Once "alternative" bands like Nirvana (see page 84) and R.E.M. (see page 72) became the biggest bands in the world, then you had to wonder what that description usefully meant any more. For my purposes, I'm leaving these terms deliberately vague but I will say that for me "cult," "alternative," and "indie" all represent the spirit in which the music is made—that punk philosophy (but not exclusive to punk) of following your own instincts and making music as a voyage of discovery and self-expression. Prince (see page 60) was a mainstream pop star but he was also a restless, impulsive innovator who forged his own path. So he's in.

Don't mistake this as a comprehensive guide to music, though. I've tried to cover most of the relevant genres, taking in dance and hip-hop, as well as boys with guitars, but my choices have also been dictated by who I was excited about drawing and writing about. I've not included anyone who I don't think is worth your ears, so there are one or two notable omissions from the standard "alternative" roster. Of which I will say to my editor: thank you for not making me write about The Libertines. There's also just not enough space to include everyone, and this has necessitated some painful decisions. Suede are one of those bands who lit my musical touchpaper in the early '90s, yet somehow they haven't made the cut. And I could (and perhaps will) make a whole book about Luke Haines in his various musical incarnations but, sadly, he's not in this one.

Still, let's not dwell too long on who didn't make it into the book and instead celebrate the 100 musicians who did. Contained herein you will find 100 illustrations and written profiles of the great and good of alternative music, with a particular focus on artists from the US and the UK, but also representatives from Canada, France, Australia, and Iceland. I hope that even if you're a fully fledged music geek, you'll still find a few new artists or albums to give a listen. I'm sure that a few incorrect facts will have crept into these potted histories, but I hope that on the whole they are truthful

and entertaining. In the event that I've got anything wrong, please rest assured that no malice was meant. Even if I'm occasionally sardonic, these are affectionate portraits of artists who have made our world sonically richer. Many of them are still active musicians, while some have long since shuffled off. Three more have died between the first edition of this book in 2016 and the updated version you hold in your hands.I hope that no more will join them in the short time-lapse between me writing this and its publication. In the past few weeks a handful of dormant bands have released new material and it's possible that other bands will release new music before this book hits the bookshelves.

That's the nature of writing about something as dynamic as music. It never stands still. Even though the music business has changed beyond recognition, artists old and new keep on creating. Of course, it's easier to look back at previous decades and decide which music has stood the test of time. The 2010s are so fresh that they've not yet settled down into the musical hindsight of previous decades (at least for me). Perhaps perversely then I've allocated proportionally fewer places to that section.I've also played a little fast and loose with decades on a few occasions. For example, The Flaming Lips (see page 108) have been going since the early '80s, but I put them in the Millennium chapter because that's when they broke through to their current status as internationally renowned space cadets. Please be kind, pedants.

Ok, shall we get on with it? Get your record player/stereo/streaming service**/MP3 player/gramophone warmed up and then turn the page. Let's look at some pretty pictures and talk music. Friends, lend me your ears!

John Riordan
London, 2020

*Of course, I realize now that there are no bad genres of music, just bad music. There's lots of jazz and classical music that I've grown to love, but like most kids I was a little philistine.

** To make things really easy for you, I have created a playlist containing a song by each of the artists profiled (apart from one or two refuseniks). You can access the playlist with either of the following links:
Spotify: sptfy.com/1kH4
Deezer: deezer.com/playlist/1863553422

CHAPTER ONE

THE Seventies STAGE

FEATURING THE FOLLOWING ARTISTS:

BLONDIE
DAVID BOWIE
joni mitchell
Nick Drake
BLACK SABBATH
LOU REED
IGGY POP
RAMONES
THE CLASH
SEX PISTOLS
BUZZCOCKS
Elvis Costello

TOM WAITS
Neil Young
Patti Smith
DEVO
Chic
ROXY MUSIC
TALKING HEADS
Parliament & FUNKADELIC
KRAFTWERK
WIRE
THE SPECIALS

★ PUNK ★ NEW WAVE ★ FOLK ★ ROCK ★ GLAM ★

BLONDIE

Like the Ramones, Blondie married their love of '60s pop with the new sound of punk but, unlike the Ramones, they actually became pop stars.

From the opening seconds of debut album Blondie (1976), the band evoked a retro world of radio pop, girl groups, and teenage crushes. Debbie Harry's spoken introduction to "X Offender" deliberately echoed the bad-boyfriend laments of The Shangri-Las. Debbie Harry's blonde bombshell looks didn't hurt either, helping to conjure a romantic pop-art atmosphere.

The band was centered on musical and romantic couple Debbie Harry (vocals) and Chris Stein (guitar). Like other artists of the punk era, Blondie were favorites at legendary New York nightspot CBGB, but they made their first popular breakthrough in the UK, where cover version "Denis" and "(I'm Always Touched by Your) Presence, Dear" from 1978's *Plastic Letters* were chart hits.

It was third album *Parallel Lines* (1978) that established them in their home country and brought them worldwide success. The album is new wave classic after classic ("Hanging on the Telephone," "One Way or Another," "Picture This," "Sunday Girl") all wrapped up in an iconic sleeve. Disco-tastic "Heart of Glass" was a global smash and showed that, like The Clash (see page 20), they were unafraid to explore new musical terrain.

They continued to write and release great material over the following two albums, *Eat to the Beat* (1979) and *Autoamerican* (1980). The latter includes the reggae cover The Tide is High" and "Rapture," which was the first US Number One to feature rapping.

Blondie broke up after their poorly received fifth album, *The Hunter* (1982). Harry went on to release solo records and sing with The Jazz Passengers. Blondie reformed in 1997, supplementing Harry, Stein, and drummer Clem Burke with additional musicians.

Their most recent album *Pollinator* (2017) features guest performances from Joan Jett and songwriting by TV On the Radio's Dave Sitek (see page 111) and Johnny Marr (see page 46) among others. Its title was inspired by Harry's recent interest in beekeeping.

TOP ALBUM *Eat to the Beat* (1979) It may not be as perfect as *Parallel Lines*, but it contains my favorite Blondie song "Union City Blues" and the mighty "Atomic," on which they continued their foray onto the dance floor. The CD reissue includes a frankly bizarre live version of Johnny Cash's "Ring of Fire."

POP TRIVIA Around the time of Blondie's breakup, Chris Stein was diagnosed with the autoimmune disease pemphigus and Harry took a few years off in the mid-1980s to care for him. Original bass player, Gary Valentine, is now better known as Gary Lachman, a writer on popular culture and the occult.

DAVID BOWIE

David Bowie was one of the most influential artists in pop music and the man who set the standard for being cool in the 1970s (and losing it in the '80s). A large part of his appeal comes from his restless reinvention, you might say the many ch-ch-changes that he put himself through.

A brief description of Bowie's career might go something like this: second-rate mod, skewed music hall entertainer, hippy guitar strummer, androgynous king of glam, plastic soul man, coked-up and spooked-out in LA, getting clean and weird in Berlin, clowning about with New Romantics, big hair and bigger pay cheque in the '80s, Jareth the Goblin King, being weird again with Brian Eno, scary rave uncle, elder statesman of Art Rock, retirement, surprise come-back... and surprise departure from the planet.

Despite this perpetual shape-shifting, it's the Bowie of the early '70s who is burned into the public cultural consciousness—Bowie as the androgynous, alien, rock 'n' roll messiah Ziggy Stardust and on the cover of *Aladdin Sane*

(1973), with his lightning-bolt makeup. These iconic looks perfectly suited the music that Bowie and his band were making: a bold, swaggering take on rock 'n' roll infused with science fiction, cabaret, pop art, and avant-garde literature. The costumes and stagecraft generated youthful adoration and adult disapproval in equal measure. A generation of impressionable youths felt something shift in their brains (and stir in their loins).

The '70s were an incredible purple patch for Bowie. His early '70s albums, *Hunky Dory* (1971), *The Rise and Fall of Ziggy Stardust and the Spiders from Mars* (1972), and *Aladdin Sane* (1973), are rightly lauded as classics. Perhaps held in even higher esteem these days are his "Berlin" albums, *Low* (1977) and *Heroes* (1977). Bowie moved to West Berlin in 1976, trying to escape from a cocaine-addled, paranoid period living in LA (captured in the record *Station to Station*). In Berlin he became inspired, newly experimental, and prolific, making two albums with Iggy Pop (see page 18) and collaborating on his own records with Tony Visconti and experimental brain-box Brian Eno (see page 33). *Low*, in particular, shows the influence of "Krautrock" bands Kraftwerk (see page 38) and Neu!. Its songs are angular and brittle, complex, and yet seemingly minimalist. *Low*'s first side features strange pop songs with gnomic lyrics (including "Sound and Vision"). The second side dispenses with lyrics all together, apart from Bowie's operatic nonsense-language, which soars over the classical/jazz/electronic landscapes of "Warszawa" and "Subterraneans."

Bowie is justly held up as a figurehead of musical innovation, but it's equally true that he was always a musical magpie, a trend-grabber as much as a trendsetter. Bowie was a cultural straddler, with one foot in the avant-garde and one foot firmly planted in the world of pop entertainment.

He appeared to have retired from music in the mid-noughties, but on Bowie's birthday, January 8, 2013, the world woke up to a new song, the melancholic "Where Are We Now?". Amazingly, Bowie, Visconti, and a handful of trusted musicians had managed to record an album in secret and *The Next Day* was released in March 2013.

On January 8, 2016, he released jazz-inflected masterpiece *Blackstar* and for two days Bowie fans marveled at this strange new album, recorded by a man who had just turned 69. Two days later we woke up to the news that Bowie had passed away from liver cancer. He had pulled off the unthinkable once more, recording a top-notch album and working on the off-Broadway musical Lazarus, while keeping his illness secret from all but a close few. Bowie's influence on music and culture in general is impossible to overstate and *Blackstar* is a *memento mori* masterpiece. Twitter wags have joked that since Bowie's death we have slipped into a cosmically dystopian parallel universe. They might just be right.

BOWIE'S MOST UNDERRATED RECORDS Bowie fans change their minds about their favorite record all the time, but here are some records that deserve more attention than they get:

Lodger (1979) The third in the so-called Berlin Trilogy, *Lodger* is eclectic to the point of being all over the place, but its exuberant experimentalism throws up some great moments, including "DJ" (containing a mystifying allusion to 1950s' UK comics hero Dan Dare) and "Red Money," in which Bowie et al rework a backing track from Iggy Pop's "Sister Midnight," recorded two years earlier. I guess it was still lying around the studio!

Absolute Beginners (1986) One of Bowie's loveliest stand-alone singles, this was apparently thrown together quickly with a crack team of session musicians, all of whom received instructions that they would be recording with a mystery "Mr X"!

The Laughing Gnome (1967) Hearing this track after Bowie's later world-changing stuff makes it seem all the weirder. It's an early, novelty comedy song from when David was still, er, finding his way. Go on, let *The Laughing Gnome* into your record collection and enjoy the excruciating puns.

POP TRIVIA *Diamond Dogs* (1974) is Bowie's great album of shelved ideas, and features the remnants of two ambitious plans. The first, to make a film set in a post-apocalyptic cityscape populated by feral gangs on roller-skates, was eventually boiled down to the title track. The second was to adapt George Orwell's novel *1984* into a musical. Orwell's widow refused to give permission, though, and songs from this project ended up on the record.

Living in Los Angeles in the mid-1970s, Bowie apparently subsisted on cocaine, red bell peppers, and milk. He was obsessed with the occult and Kabbalah, believed that witches were stealing his, erm, personal fluids, and supposedly kept his urine in jars in the refrigerator. Fortunately for us, he channeled this mental anguish into the sinister masterpiece "Station to Station," on the 1975 album of the same name.

Arthouse auteur Nic Roeg cast Bowie as Jerome Newton, the stranded, alien protagonist of *The Man Who Fell to Earth* (1976). Bowie returned to this character at the end of his life, casting Michael C. Hall as Newton in the off-Broadway musical *Lazarus*.

joni mitchell

Born in Canada, Joni Mitchell moved to California in the early 1970s and became a major musical voice of the hippy, bohemian counterculture.

Joni Mitchell's music is often built around intricate, fingerpicked guitar arrangements, incorporating unusual tunings. Equally distinctive is her trilling voice, darting between joy, sadness, and social comment in Mitchell's poetic lyrics.

Mitchell was championed (and covered) early on by The Byrds' David Crosby. Her breakthrough album was *Ladies of the Canyon* (1970), which featured generational anthem "Woodstock" and environmental toe-tapper "Big Yellow Taxi." Her following albums, *Blue* (1971), *For the Roses* (1972), and *Court and Spark* (1974) managed the rare feat of being both critical and commercial hits. On later albums she moved further away from her folky beginnings, exploring jazz textures and arrangements with collaborators that included Charles Mingus and Herbie Hancock. In the '80s she recorded albums that verged on synth-pop.

Joni Mitchell has been a huge influence on musicians as varied as Joanna Newsom (see page 128) and Sonic Youth's Thurston Moore (see page 43) , who has attributed his band's unusual guitar tunings to her influence and dedicated a song to her, "Hey Joni."

In 2015, Mitchell suffered a brain aneurysm but has apparently recovered well with the help of physical therapy. In November 2018, she attended Both Sides Now, a concert celebrating her 75th birthday and her music.

TOP ALBUM *Blue* (1971) This is perhaps her most confessional album and still considered by many to be her classic. Lyrically, it includes references to the baby girl that she gave up for adoption in 1965, although this didn't become public knowledge until the '90s.

POP TRIVIA Joni Mitchell is an accomplished painter and many of her album sleeves feature her artwork. In June 2000 she described herself to Toronto's *The Globe and Mail* as a "painter derailed by circumstance."

Nick Drake

Poor Nick Drake—sometimes the public just doesn't get it until it's too late.

Nick Drake released only three albums in his tragically short life, but they are a near-perfect body of work, suffused with a very English spirit of folky melancholia. The constants of Drake's music are his remarkable acoustic guitar-playing, plaintive voice, and poetic, ambiguous lyrics.

He and his producers tried different approaches on each album, in part searching for a sound that would connect with a largely indifferent public. *Five Leaves Left* (1969) is all pastoral folk guitar, supported by lush string and woodwind arrangements. *Bryter Layter* (1971) has a jazzier feel, with drums, bass, and backing vocals, and includes the beautiful "Northern Sky" (which features John Cale on piano and celeste.) In contrast, 1972's *Pink Moon* is stripped back to just Drake and his guitar (apart from a hint of piano on the title track). This was partly a reaction against what Drake considered to be the overcomplicated production of Bryter Layter, but also reflected his increasing depression and sense of alienation.

Drake's lack of commercial success was not helped by his chronic shyness and dislike of playing live. After *Pink Moon*, he returned to live with his parents at his childhood home in Warwickshire. He recorded four more songs in 1974, including the haunting "Black Eyed Dog," a stark, poetic description of his depression.

Nick Drake died on November 25, 1974, aged 26, from an overdose of antidepressant pills. His death was officially recorded as suicide, although it is not known whether he intended to take his life. Since his death his popularity and influence have grown and grown, in part due to name-checks from other musicians, including Robert Smith of The Cure (see page 54), Peter Buck of R.E.M. (see page 72), and Graham Coxon of Blur (see page 78).

TOP ALBUMS Honestly, you might as well listen to all three. *Pink Moon* is only 28 minutes long! Follow them up with 2004's *Made to Love Magic* for the complete picture, including those last four recorded songs and alternative versions of earlier songs.

POP TRIVIA At school at Marlborough College in the '60s, Drake formed a band with the incredible name of The Perfumed Gardeners. Apparently, fellow pupil Chris De Burgh asked to join the band but was rejected on musical grounds.

BLACK SABBATH

Four lads from Birmingham formed a rock band and accidentally invented heavy metal.

Ozzy Osbourne is undoubtedly the most famous member of Black Sabbath—although these days he is as famous for being a shambling househusband as a satanic rock star—but the chief songwriters of Black Sabbath were guitarist Tony Iommi and bass player Geezer Butler. Drummer Bill Ward completed the original line-up.

The band formed as a heavy blues-rock band in 1968 under the name of Earth. Discovering that there was already a band called Earth, they renamed themselves Black Sabbath after a Boris Karloff horror film. Iommi came up with the riff for the song of the same name, incorporating the tritone or "Devil's Interval" (a musical interval comprising of three whole tones, which was supposedly banned by the medieval church), while Butler and Osbourne wrote the lyrics, drawing on the books of Dennis Wheatley and an unnerving nocturnal vision Butler had of a dark figure lurking at the foot of his bed. The song went down so well with live audiences that it changed the band's direction and image.

Their first album, *Black Sabbath* (1970), contains the title song and other tales of wizards, nightmares, and the Devil. Recorded in two days and an instant hit, the band followed it up the same year with second album *Paranoid*, which contains some of their most popular songs: "War Pigs," "Iron Man," and title track "Paranoid." These two albums established the musical template of Black Sabbath—seriously chunky riffs topped by Osbourne's soulful, bluesy voice. There's a kind of idiot brilliance about Sabbath at their best. Subtle, it ain't, but it's great fun, and not always about witches and warlocks. "Paranoid" is the singer explaining that he's had to split up with his girlfriend because he's gone insane (possibly the best excuse for dumping someone ever).

Fear of insanity is an ongoing lyrical obsession in the following albums, which is perhaps understandable given the incredible amounts of booze and drugs that the band were shoveling into themselves. For a few years they managed to maintain the hedonistic lifestyle and the quality of the music. They stretched their (demonic) wings on *Master of Reality* (1971) and *Vol. 4* (1972), which included acoustic instrumental numbers, while *Sabbath Bloody Sabbath* (1973) featured strings, synths, and Rick Wakeman from Yes (although, obviously, it was written in a dungeon).

Eventually the drink and drugs took their toll. Osbourne was fired from the band in 1979 and Black Sabbath played and recorded with a succession of singers, including Rainbow's Ronnie James Dio. In the 1980s and '90s the band continued with multiple line-ups, the only constant presence being Iommi. The four original members re-united in 1997 and released the live album *Reunion*. In 2013, Ozzy Osbourne, Tony Iommi, and Geezer Butler released Black Sabbath's 19th studio album *13*. In 2016, the band embarked on "The End" tour, performing their final (probably) concert in Birmingham in February 2017. Black Sabbath disbanded soon after, but Osbourne has speculated about reforming for one-off gigs, possibly for the Commonwealth Games, which are due to take place in Birmingham in 2022.

TOP ALBUM *Paranoid* (1970) There's plenty of good stuff on later albums, but this one's hard to top. It's got the insane genius of the title track, the serious riffage of "Iron Man," and songs called "Rat Salad" and "Fairies Wear Boots." What more do you want?

POP TRIVIA The band's manager (and dad of Sharon Osbourne) Don Arden commissioned a piece of stage furniture based on the megaliths of Stonehenge. Unfortunately, there was a mix-up between feet and meters, and the resulting prop was too massive to fit on the stage. Incredibly, this does not appear to be the inspiration for a similar scenario in the film *This is Spinal Tap* (1984), in which the Stonehenge monument is made too small. The Black Sabbath gaffe occurred on their 1983 tour and the Spinal Tap joke was already included in a "demo" version of the film made for financiers in 1982.

LOU REED

Lou Reed was the acerbic vampire of New York City, who inspired legions of music fans to dress in black, wear sunglasses indoors, and hang around on street corners looking moody.

Reed made it his mission to write about the underbelly of city life—the seedy, dispossessed, drug-addicted, and marginalized. His songs were populated by junkies and weirdos, as well as homosexuals and transsexuals, in an era when they were booted to the fringes of society. As lyricist for The Velvet Underground he realized that, unlike literature, rock refused to touch these risqué subjects, and so he made them his own. It was, he said, "like shooting fish in a barrel."

The Velvet Underground went on to be hugely influential, but at the time had only a small cult following. Brian Eno famously said that the Velvet's first album sold only 30,000 records in five years, but that "everyone who bought one of those 30,000 copies started a band." (Actually, 30,000 sounds pretty good by today's standards.) One of those cult fans was David Bowie (see page 10) who in '70s star-maker mode (see also Iggy Pop, page 18) persuaded Reed to let him produce his 1972 album *Transformer*. Bowie's golden touch and Mick Ronson's lush arrangements opened up a more accessible side of Reed's songs and *Transformer* became an unlikely commercial success. "Walk on the Wild Side," affectionately recalling transgressive members of Andy Warhol's Factory setup, became the signature song of Reed's career, and one he sometimes found hard to escape.

He followed *Transformer* with *Berlin* (1973), a dark concept album about Jim and Caroline, two doomed junkies. It was panned at the time of release, but is now considered a miserablist classic. *Berlin* is fantastically over the top, so much so that it sometimes veers into unintentional comedy. Amid epic strings, honking horns, and cabaret piano, he speaksings of drugs, prostitution, domestic abuse, and suicide. "The Kids" ends with the sound of Caroline's children screaming for their mother as they are taken away by the authorities.

Reed and The Velvet Underground were a big influence on the New York punk crowd, centered on the venues CBGB and Max's Kansas City in the mid- to late '70s. Though he publicly disassociated himself from punk, he played occasional gigs with Patti Smith (see page 28) and Talking Heads' David Byrne (see page 34).

Throughout the 1980s, 1990s, and 2000s, Reed carried on recording albums to varying levels of commercial and critical success. These include 1989's accessible *New York*, 2003's *The Raven*, a star-studded musical adaptation of the work of Edgar Allan Poe, and his final album, *Lulu* (2011), a collaboration with heavy metal band Metallica. In 1990 he reunited with The Velvet Underground's John Cale to make *Songs for Drella*, a concept album about their former mentor, Andy Warhol. The Velvet Underground briefly reformed to tour Europe in 1993.

Lou Reed died of liver failure in New York in 2013, survived by his wife, the performance artist and singer Laurie Anderson.

TOP ALBUM For an accessible entry point to Lou Reed, try his 1975 album *Metal Machine Music*.

Only kidding, it's an hour of unlistenable-to, atonal madness, and was either recorded as a "f*** you" to his record company at the time, or is Lou indulging his most experimental urges, depending on who you believe. Let's go for *Take No Prisoners* (1978). This live album finds Reed and band on great form, as he abuses and entertains the crowd with long, witty ad-libs.

POP TRIVIA It's fair to say that Lou Reed had a difficult relationship with his parents. Worried by his teenage behavior they consented to him receiving electroconvulsive therapy. Reed wrote about this disturbing experience in "Kill Your Sons," from 1974's *Sally Can't Dance*.

IGGY POP

These days Iggy Pop is the much-loved godfather of alternative music, an international treasure with his own radio show on BBC 6 Music. But let's not forget that he forged his musical reputation as the wild man of rock.

David Bowie, that most calculated of pop stars, was drawn to him because he saw in Pop the trailer-trash, Dionysian spirit of rock 'n' roll. As frontman of proto-punks The Stooges, he was infamous for his self-destructive habits and confrontational behavior on stage. The Stooges released two albums of their primitive garage rock, *The Stooges* (1969) and *Funhouse* (1970), before splitting up. They were persuaded to reform as Iggy and the Stooges for the Bowie-produced *Raw Power* (1973). All these albums sold poorly at the time, but subsequently had a huge influence on punk, grunge, and alternative rock.

In 1976 Pop accompanied Bowie to Europe where they tried to kick their respective drug habits and worked on new music. This period of collaboration with Bowie, Tony Visconti, and Bowie's band produced two highly acclaimed albums, *The Idiot* and *Lust for Life*, both released in 1977. The latter album features two of his best-known songs, "The Passenger" and "Lust for Life."

In the 1980s, 1990s, and 2000s Pop embraced his position as a founding father of alternative rock, playing with many of the punk and alternative musicians he had influenced, including Steve Jones of the Sex Pistols (see page 22), Chris Stein and Clem Burke from Blondie (see page 9), Green Day, and Death in Vegas.

In 2003, the surviving original members of The Stooges, Ron and Scott Asheton, performed on Pop's album *Skull Ring*. His 2016 album, *Post Pop Depression* was a collaboration with Josh Homme of Queens of the Stone Age (see page 110). Perhaps with a tip of the hat to Bowie's *Blackstar*, Pop released a jazz-inflected album *Free* in 2019, based around collaborations with trumpeter and composer Leron Thomas.

TOP ALBUM *The Idiot* (1977) This may not represent the rockier side of Pop, but it contains some of his most fascinating songs. "Sister Midnight" is a funky, Oedipal nightmare in which he tries to work out some, erm, parent issues. "Dum Dum Boys" is the story of The Stooges, retold to darkly comic effect. And perhaps best of all is "Mass Production," in which Mr. Pop's libido collides with a nightmarish evocation of America as a relentless factory.

POP TRIVIA Iggy Pop's street cred took a bit of a dent in the UK in 2009 when he appeared in a series of TV adverts with a puppet "mini-me" for insurance company Swiftcover. In his 2014 John Peel Lecture for the BBC he explained that he had filmed the ads in order to finance future music releases.

RAMONES

The sound of the Ramones is recognizable in an instant—relentless fuzz guitar played at breakneck speed, underpinned by propulsive bass and drums, and topped off with Joey's street-mangled vocals.

The band formed in Queens, New York, in 1974. Bass player and main songwriter Dee Dee got the Ramones name from an early Paul McCartney pseudonym, Paul Ramon, and the band members all adopted this as their surname: Joey Ramone (vocals), Johnny Ramone (guitar), Dee Dee Ramone (bass), and Tommy Ramone (drums). The Ramones' frantic playing style and uniform (leather jackets, skinny jeans) set them apart from contemporary bands and, once they became regulars at legendary New York venue CBGB, their sound helped set the template for punk.

The classic Ramones' songs are an exercise in economy (the longest song on their debut clocks in at 2 minutes 40 seconds) and meaningful simplicity. The band settled on a deliberately basic, direct playing style and created a huge number of songs from these seemingly limited elements. Their first three albums, *Ramones* (1976), *Leave Home* (1977), and *Rocket to Russia* (1977), are stuffed with punk-pop classics, including "Blitzkrieg Bop," "Pinhead," "Rockaway Beach," and "Sheena is a Punk Rocker."

The band was popular in London before their native New York. Playing at London's Roundhouse in 1977, they met members of the Sex Pistols (see page 22) and The Clash (page 20), and influenced the nascent UK punk scene. The Ramones were themselves influenced by proto-punks The Stooges (see page 18) and MC5, but also by '60s pop such as the Beach Boys and girl groups like The Shangri-las. The bubblegum pop aspect of their sound came to the fore when they recorded End of the Century (1980) with producer (and gun-toting maniac) Phil Spector.

The Ramones continued to tour and record throughout the '80s and '90s, before finally calling it a day in 1996. All four original Ramones have since passed away.

TOP ALBUM *Ramones* (1976) It's all there from the first few bars of "Blitzkrieg Bop." The sound, the attitude, the snotty vocals, the chanted intermissions, the pop hooks. The Ramones seemed to emerge fully formed, complete with iconic cover shoot of the band as artfully ragged street urchins leaning against a brick wall, an image copied by every guitar band since.

POP TRIVIA As chronicled in the brilliant 2003 documentary *End of the Century*, Dee Dee Ramone left the band in 1989 and briefly reinvented himself as a rapper. He never rejoined the Ramones, although, confusingly, he continued to write songs for them.

THE CLASH

It's been said that The Clash were the punk band that liked to say "yes." Whereas other punks growled a nihilistic "no" to anything that wasn't dressed in bondage trousers, The Clash embraced new styles of music and culture with enthusiasm and genuine interest. This included reggae, dub, and on later albums funk and hip-hop.

This open attitude extended to the world beyond rock hedonism. Joe Strummer, in particular, also brought a political attitude to his lyrics, writing about inequality and social deprivation. In retrospect it's easy to deride The Clash for being naïve or for mixing their idealistic politics with pop-star posing, but by the standards of rock music (not given to lengthy explorations of realpolitik) their political stance was fairly coherent. Pop music is a language of broad gestures suited to idealistic declarations and, much like Public Enemy (see page 68), Strummer et al inspired music fans to educate themselves and broaden their cultural horizons.

The Clash arrived on the music scene with a splash, wearing paint-spattered clothing bearing agitprop slogans. In fact, they emerged from the same London punky soup as the Sex Pistols (see page 22). Their first manager, Bernie Rhodes, was friends with punk pioneer and Sex Pistols' manager Malcolm McLaren, while their original rhythm guitarist, Keith Levine, later played with John Lydon in PiL. Terry Chimes played drums on debut album *The Clash* (1977), but by the second album, *Give 'Em Enough Rope* (1978), the line-up had settled down as Joe Strummer (vocals and rhythm guitar), Mick Jones (lead guitar and occasional vocals), Paul Simonon (bass), and Topper Headon (drums).

With the exception of the cover of Junior Murvin's "Police and Thieves" and the swinging "Julie's Been Working for the Drug Squad," the first two albums are fairly straightforward punk. It's on 1979's *London Calling* that things get interesting. It's a smorgasbord of musical styles, showing the band playing with their influences, from the ska-inflected "Rudie Can't Fail" and "Wrong 'em Boyo" to the dub-heavy (and much sampled) "Guns of Brixton" via the Morricone-twang of "Spanish Bombs" (Strummer channeling Spanish poet Lorca) and faux-classical fanfares of "The Card Cheat." Despite its title, *London Calling* also shows the band rejecting their putative anti-Americanism ("I'm So Bored of the USA") and embracing American rock 'n' roll, rockabilly, and jazz.

The band's magpie ambition overshot itself on 1980's triple-album *Sandinista*, although it did produce some thrilling results (see below). 1982's *Combat Rock* continued to explore dubby, effects-heavy textures, notably on the gorgeous "Straight to Hell." It also produced the band's two big crossover hits, "Rock the Casbah" and "Should I Stay or Should I Go?".

Topper Headon left the band in 1982 and in 1983 Strummer fired Mick Jones. Strummer and Simonon struggled on with other musicians to release *Cut the Crap* (1985), an album now considered so bad that it has been deleted and all but airbrushed from the band's history.

Mick Jones went on to start Big Audio Dynamite with filmmaker and DJ Don Letts. The band continued The Clash's mission of cultural cross-pollination by combining rock, dance music, hip-hop, and reggae with extensive use of samples. Joe Strummer eventually returned to touring and recording with his band The Mescaleros. In 2002, he died from an undiagnosed heart defect at the age of 50.

TOP ALBUM *Sandinista!* (1980) I have a soft spot for ramshackle follies and this bloated, 36-song, triple-album is The Clash's. It starts with the seriously funky "The Magnificent Seven," then moves into Motown pastiche with "Hitsville U.K." From there on in it's anyone's guess where they'll head next. It takes in rockabilly, disco, folk, swing, carnival, gospel, and, of course, reggae. Suffice it to say that things get pretty dubby and I imagine it was pretty smoky in the studio.

POP TRIVIA Venerable Beat poet Allen Ginsberg makes a guest appearance on *Combat Rock*. On "Ghetto Defendant" he trades abstruse lyrics with Strummer about heroin addiction, the poet Rimbaud, and South American politics.

SEX PISTOLS

Musicologists of the 25th century will still be debating whether punk started in the US or the UK, but one thing is certain—the Sex Pistols were the sneering, gob-speckled face of punk in Britain.

The band formed in 1975 but, as far as the Great British public was concerned, they emerged as fully formed Antichrists in 1976 with the ferocious single "Anarchy in the UK." The Sex Pistols burned brightly and briefly, releasing only one studio album, *Never Mind the Bollocks, Here's the Sex Pistols* (1977),

before falling apart in spectacular, self-loathing acrimony. By 1979 punk figurehead Sid Vicious was dead (as was his girlfriend Nancy Spungen) and John Lydon was locked in a legal battle with manager Malcolm McLaren for monies owed and the use of the name "Johnny Rotten."

The Sex Pistols were arguably the last band to inspire moral panic of the "Ban this filth!" variety. The British press went to town, politicians called for their arrest, and the Pistols found themselves in the strange position of being a famous band who could rarely play live, as few venues would have them. Julien Temple's excellent 2000 documentary *The Filth and the Fury* does an excellent job of placing the Pistols' rebellious rise in the context of moribund, exhausted Britain in the '70s. Their "anarchist" politics may have been half-arsed, but Johnny Rotten's furious cries of "No future!" struck a genuine chord with a nation's disillusioned youth.

The revolution was musical as well as political. Punk rebelled against the self-indulgent excesses of '70s rock, the prog concept albums, and the '60s stars who had become the new mainstream. Hence the punk truism: "Never trust a hippy." In fact, the Pistols' music owed a lot to '50s rock 'n' roll, '60s bands like The Who, and proto-punks The Stooges (see page 18).

Things came to a head with the release of the single "God Save the Queen" in May 1977, timed to coincide with Queen Elizabeth II's Silver Jubilee. The song—as well as Jamie Reid's icon-busting cover—were too much for the British, kowtowing establishment. The song was banned from BBC and independent radio, and the UK chart was (probably) rigged so that the single placed second after Rod Stewart.

After the Pistols split up, John Lydon formed ever-mutating post-punk band Public Image Ltd (PiL). In 1996, the Sex Pistols reformed, with original bass player Glen Matlock, for the teasingly titled Filthy Lucre tour and have played together periodically since. They have continued to annoy punk purists by releasing a Sex Pistols-branded credit card and perfume.

TOP ALBUMS *Never Mind the Bollocks, Here's the Sex Pistols* (1977) Their only studio album holds up well 40 years later, both as a collection of rock songs and as a social record. All the great, rabble-rousing songs are here—"Anarchy in the UK," "Pretty Vacant," "Holidays in the Sun,"—propelled by Steve Jones' meaty guitar and Paul Cook's powerful drumming. It's a bit one-note, but then you don't really want to hear the Sex Pistols doing a ballad, do you?

The Great Rock 'n' Roll Swindle (1979) Speaking of which, here's your chance to hear Sid Vicious tackle "My Way." *The Great Rock 'n' Roll Swindle* almost qualifies as a Sex Pistols' album, being a ragtag collection of songs culled from the film of the same name, initiated by McClaren and finished by Julien Temple. Listening to Sid attempting to mug his way through Johnny B. Goode, despite knowing almost none of the lyrics, is a painful experience.

POP TRIVIA Glen Matlock was the original bass player and co-wrote some of their early songs. He was apparently kicked out of the band for liking The Beatles too much (although this is probably an example of Malcolm McLaren writing a good sound bite). The rest of the band allegedly amused themselves by doing unspeakable things to Matlock's sandwiches when he wasn't looking (this is also probably not true).

John Lydon's strangest career choice was advertising Country Life butter on UK TV in 2008. He was much criticized but has said that the ad money paid for him to make subsequent PiL albums. Still, given the rumors about Matlock's sandwiches, it's probably best to decline if Johnny Rotten offers you a well-buttered roll.

IT LOOKS LIKE YOU'RE TRYING TO START A REBELLIOUS YOUTH MOVEMENT...

WOULD YOU LIKE SOME HELP?

...ANARCHYYY!

BUZZCOCKS

Buzzcocks (there's no "the") are like a very English version of the Ramones. They specialize in bittersweet laments of the heart, wrapped in throwaway pop tunes and delivered by frantic punk guitars.

The band was formed in Manchester in 1976 by Pete Shelley and Howard Devoto. Although they had already been playing in an embryonic version of the band, it was a trip to London to see the Sex Pistols that fired them up with punk energy. They organized the Pistols' first Manchester gig at the Lesser Free Trade Hall in June 1976, an event that seemingly every future face on the Manchester music scene attended.

In 1979 they released the *Spiral Scratch* EP, an energetic collection of songs, including "Boredom," which was roughly recorded by legendary producer Martin Hannett. Significantly, they released the record themselves, becoming the first punk band to do so. Howard Devoto left the band soon after, later to found post-punk band Magazine. Pete Shelley took over lead vocals and Steve Diggle moved from bass to second guitar.

Buzzcocks released the brilliantly titled *Another Music in a Different Kitchen* in 1978 and followed this up with *Love Bites* in the same year and *A Different Kind of Tension* in 1979.

Though the songs are played at breakneck speed, their sound and lyrical concerns set them apart from their punk contemporaries. Pete Shelley's high, reedy singing voice is precision-tuned for complaint and a Buzzcocks' song is much more likely to be about romantic disappointment than an aggressive state-of-the-nation polemic. Shelley's bisexuality arguably gave him an additional outsider's perspective on the macho world of rock music, and in songs like "Fiction Romance" and "What Do I Get?"—three-minute anthems for romantic losers—he creates pop poetry out of the common experience of heartache.

Buzzcocks broke up in 1981 but have reformed a few times over the years, featuring Shelley and Diggle backed by various musicians. They released their last album *The Way* in 2014. Pete Shelley died in 2018, but the band continue with Diggle on lead vocals.

TOP ALBUM *Love Bites* (1979) This is chock-full of great songs, including pop-punk masterpiece "Ever Fallen In Love (With Someone You Shouldn't've)", minimalist gem "E.S.P.," and lovely instrumental "Walking Distance."

POP TRIVIA Steve Diggle bears an uncanny resemblance to deceased Irish poet Seamus Heaney. It's true, google them both!

Elvis Costello

Elvis Costello was an unlikely pop star in the late 1970s and '80s, an articulate and clever British songwriter whose name and geeky look referenced two of the icons of American rock 'n' roll: Elvis Presley and Buddy Holly.

Like Joe Strummer (see page 20), Costello (real name Declan MacManus) came up through the London pub rock scene. Although his breakthrough was contemporary with punk, he was never really punk in style or temperament. His debut record, *My Aim Is True* (1977), proudly flaunts its classic R&B influences married to Costello's snappy lyrics. He recruited a backing band, The Attractions, to record *This Year's Model* (1978), which included the UK singles "Pump It Up" and "(I Don't Want to Go to) Chelsea." In 1979 he honed his songwriting further on *Armed Forces*, which featured his biggest hit "Oliver's Army," a chart-pleasing, melodic tune with savage lyrics about British colonialism, the Troubles in Northern Ireland, and working class prospects.

Costello has made albums that draw on soul, country, and jazz, and he has collaborated with musicians such as Paul McCartney, Burt Bacharach, the Brodsky Quartet, and The Roots. His 2018 album *Look Now* included songs co-written with Burt Bacharach and Carole King. In retrospect, Costello's career looks like a pretty thorough exploration of 20th-century music, or of popular music in the broadest sense.

TOP ALBUM *Armed Forces* (1979) The album's working title was "Emotional Fascism" and that should give you an idea of the combination of personal and political themes contained therein. The dense, pithy lyrics are backed up by The Attractions at their poppiest. Apparently, the band was obsessed with Abba at the time.

POP TRIVIA Elvis Costello adopted his surname from the stage name used by his dad. "Day Costello" (Ross MacManus) was a professional jazz trumpeter and singer. Costello Junior's first broadcast recording was singing backing vocals for his dad, who wrote and sang "I'm a Secret Lemonade Drinker" for a lemonade commercial. Costello has also produced records for artists including The Specials (see page 41) and The Pogues (see page 70).

TOM WAITS

Tom Waits lives in a neon-lit *demimonde* of after-hours bars, populated by one-armed dwarves and chain-smoking ladies of the night. Occasionally he finishes his glass of bourbon and allows himself to be led to the piano (or rusty glockenspiel) where he sings a song. Every few years these recordings are collated to form his new album. Probably.

Literally, as well as lyrically, Tom Waits has an amazing voice—just listen to that broken growl, full of gravel and regret. His early albums, including *Closing Time* (1973), *The Heart of Saturday Night* (1974), and *Small Change* (1976), feature sozzled jazz ballads built around piano, strings, and his cracked croon. In 1975 Waits accentuated his nightclub-singer persona by recording *Nighthawks at the Diner* in front of a small studio audience, including comic spoken preambles.

In 1980, he married screenwriter Kathleen Brennan, who he has credited as co-writer on many songs since. Brennan introduced him to the music of Captain Beefheart (although bizarrely he had shared a manager with Beefheart earlier in his career), which would have a big influence on his subsequent music. On *Swordfish*

Trombones (1983) and *Rain Dogs* (1985) he pioneered a new sound—a woozy, bluesy primitive music, seemingly played on strange broken instruments, like a drunken party in a tool shed, punctuated by spoken-word tales of sailors, weirdos, and arsonists.

Tom Waits has continued to plow this rich ground ever since, using instruments such as bagpipes, marimba, pump organ, brass, and chamberlin to create unconventional, sometimes dissonant sounds.

TOP ALBUM *Orphans: Brawlers, Bawlers and Bastards* (2006) Take a week off work and immerse yourself in Waits' bizarre world with this album; a collection of 80-plus songs divided into three themed discs. *Brawlers* features rock and blues-oriented numbers, *Bawlers* his downbeat ballads, and *Bastards* his more experimental and spoken-word material.

POP TRIVIA Perhaps because his own music is so theatrical, Waits has managed that rare knack of being a musician who is also a well-respected actor. He has appeared in films by Francis Ford Coppola, Jim Jarmusch, and Terry Gilliam, as well as playing the lead on stage in *Frank's Wild Years*, a musical play that he wrote with his wife and which grew out of the track of the same name on *Swordfishtrombones*.

Neil Young

By the start of the 1970s, Neil Young was already a veteran of Buffalo Springfield and country-rock supergroup Crosby, Stills, Nash, and Young.

Neil Young released his first solo album, *Neil Young*, in 1969 and later that year his first record with backing band Crazy Horse, *Everybody Knows This Is Nowhere*. But it was 1970's *After the Gold Rush* that was his critical and commercial breakthrough. Singing in his distinctive thin, high voice, Young touches on subjects such as environmental degradation, racism, love, and loss.

Next came *Harvest* (1972), featuring contributions by Crosby, Stills, and Nash, Linda Ronstadt, James Taylor, and the London Symphony Orchestra. *Harvest* had a mellow, country vibe with occasional rockier moments and the album's commercial success caught Young off-guard and brought him a level of fame he was uncomfortable with.

His music since has tended to oscillate between a pastoral, acoustic style and much harder rock. He's become known for long, squalling guitar solos, an aspect of his work that has been a big influence on grunge and alternative rock artists such as Nirvana (see page 84), Sonic Youth (see page 43), and Dinosaur Jr. (see page 56). In 1982 he released *Trans*, featuring vocoders, synthesizers, and other electronic beats, whose central theme of communication through technology was inspired by his son, who was unable to speak because of severe cerebral palsy. As well as being a prolific songwriter, Young is an environmental and political activist, often combining his beliefs with his music, as on his 2015 concept album *The Monsanto Years*. He has also been a longstanding critic of the audio quality of downloaded music.

TOP ALBUM *Harvest* (1972) "Heart of Gold" and the harrowing "The Needle and the Damage Done" are worth the price of admission alone. "Old Man" was written for Louis Avila, the caretaker of Young's ranch in California. Mixing the record at Young's ranch, his producer, Elliot Mazer, apparently placed one set of speakers in a barn and the other in his house. Sitting outside to review the stereo mix, Young yelled, "More barn!"

POP TRIVIA Like Bob Dylan, Young is an infamously wilful performer. Playing a concert before the release of *Tonight's the Night* (1975), he played the unreleased record to an increasingly bemused crowd. Returning to the stage for the encore, he said, "And here's one you might have heard before," and then launched back into the album's opening song.

Patti Smith

Patti Smith was a poet before she was a singer. She spent the early 1970s performing spoken-word gigs and hanging out with dirt-poor artists in New York, including photographer Robert Mapplethorpe.

By 1974, Patti Smith was making music with a band put together by guitarist Lenny Kaye. Smith mixed singing and spoken poetry over her band's loose rock structures. The Patti Smith Band's first single was a cover of rock standard "Hey Joe," with the addition of a provocative opening section in which Smith speculated as to the sexual activity of kidnapped heiress and converted revolutionary Patty Hearst. The B-side, "Piss Factory," drew on Smith's memory of time spent working on a factory assembly line and the literary salvation she found in the work of the 19th-century French poet, Arthur Rimbaud.

In 1975 the group released their debut album, *Horses*, which was produced by John Cale. Like the preceding single it opened with a cover, in this case Van Morrison's "Gloria," but with added Christian-baiting lyrics by Smith. *Horses'* combination of emphatic garage rock and wild, free, beat poetry is a bewitching brew. Patti Smith was a fixture of the CBGB's punk scene and her fierce, provocative attitude and DIY spirit certainly place her in the punk vanguard. But the music has more in common with classic American rock and garage rock. *Horses* includes songs inspired by Smith's dead rock idols, Hendrix ("Birdland") and Jim Morrison ("Break It Up").

Smith's former lover, and lifelong friend, Robert Mapplethorpe, shot the stark, black, and white cover for *Horses*. Smith's androgynous, yet sexy look was inspired by her beloved Rimbaud and the iconic photo cemented her reputation as a punk poet, as well as going on to influence the look of wannabe rock stars—both boys and girls—for decades.

The follow-up record, *Radio Ethiopia* (1976), was less accessible than its predecessor, but 1978's *Easter* included her biggest hit, "Because the Night," which was co-written with Bruce Springsteen. She made one more record, *Waves* (1979), before retiring from music for most of the '80s. She married Fred "Sonic" Smith, formerly guitar player with the MC5, and started a family. She didn't make another album until 1988's *Dream of Life*, after the birth of her second child.

After the death of her husband in 1994, Smith gradually returned to performing and music-making. She has recorded six studio albums since, campaigned for causes and groups, including the Green Party of the United States, and given lectures on Rimbaud and William Blake. She has been and continues to be a powerful role model for artistic expression and integrity, in particular for female artists.

TOP ALBUM *Easter* (1978) Patti Smith's debut album, *Horses*, is rightly lauded, but everyone's heard that one. Let's give *Easter* a spin. "Because the Night" is a corker, "Space Monkey" evolves into a pleasingly manic din, and "Babelogue" gets across the incantatory effect of Smith's freeform poetry. "Rock N Roll N-----" is well-meant but cringe-inducing, whereas the title track, appropriately enough, induces something like religious ecstasy.

POP TRIVIA In 2010, Smith won the US National Book Award for her memoir *Just Kids*, which describes her early days in New York and focuses on her relationship with Robert Mapplethorpe. Her second volume of memoir, *M Train*, was published in 2015.

DEVO

Devo's cranky, new wave art-funk has influenced many bands, but few have attempted to imitate their mischievous conceptual pranksterism.

The band started as a jokey art project by Kent State University students Gerald Casale and Bob Lewis. It was based around the concept of "de-evolution"—the idea that mankind is, in fact, regressing into animal stupidity, as evidenced by contemporary consumer culture. With keyboard player Mark Mothersbaugh, they formed a loose band and began performing at arts festivals.

The Kent State shootings of 1970, where four students were shot dead by Ohio National Guardsmen during a protest against the US invasion of Cambodia, added new impetus to their darkly humorous message. Their concerts grew increasingly confrontational, incorporating bizarre characters such as "Booji Boy," a simian mutant baby played by Mark Mothersbaugh.

In 1976, Devo won a prize for their short film *The Truth About De-Evolution,* a surreal, nightmarish film which features the band performing "Secret Agent Man" and "Jocko Homo." This brought them to the attention of David Bowie (see page 10) who persuaded Warner Bros. to sign the band. Their debut record, *Q: Are We Not Men? A: We Are Devo!* (1978), was produced by Brian Eno (see page 32) and included "Mongoloid," "Jocko Homo," and their jerky, splenetic cover of the Rolling Stones' "(I Can't Get No) Satisfaction."

Devo moved toward a more electronic, synth-pop sound with their next few albums. In 1980 they scored an unlikely hit with "Whip It" from their third album, *Freedom of Choice.* "Whip It" had a witty video which received regular airplay on MTV. Devo became known for their strange costumes. At the time of *Freedom Of Choice,* they began wearing their characteristic "energy domes"—round, ziggurat-shaped hats that they claimed recycled wasted orgone energy.

1981's *New Traditionalists* included the single "Through Being Cool,"

a reaction against the mainstream fans that "Whip It" had brought them and a celebration of nerdy outsider status. For this album they swapped the energy domes for plastic wigs modeled on the hairstyle of JFK. The look was dubbed "Utopian Boy Scout."

Devo released four more studio albums before dissolving in 1990. Since 1995 they have toured and recorded sporadically. At the time of writing their "de-evolution" concept seems increasingly convincing.

TOP ALBUM *Q: Are We Not Men? A: We Are Devo!* (1978) This is a statement of wilfully weird intent. Listen to "Jocko Homo" or "Shrivel Up" and imagine how strange they must have sounded in 1978. It also has the best album title ever.

POP TRIVIA Mark Mothersbaugh went on to become an in-demand television and film composer, most notably for *Rugrats* and Wes Anderson movies.

Chic

Chic is the sound of disco played live, not the monstrous cliché that it became, but funk's cocky, precocious little brother. The classic Chic sound is Nile Rodgers' effortlessly syncopated guitar sailing over Bernard Edwards' burbling, propulsive bass and Tony Thompson's metronomic drums.

Although they met as session musicians, Rodgers and Edwards always envisaged Chic as an actual band with a cohesive sound and image. This was partially inspired by the two of them seeing a Roxy Music (see page 32) concert in New York. To record their debut album, *Chic* (1977), they recruited Norma Jean Wright and Luci Martin to sing vocals, although they later recorded with a range of female vocalists. The album featured their first hit single, "Dance, Dance, Dance (Yowsah, Yowsah, Yowsah)."

Their second album, *C'est Chic* (1978), produced the classic song, "Le Freak." Inspired by Rodgers and Edwards being turned away from Studio 54, the song's famous refrain was originally an insult aimed at the Studio 54 doormen: "Aaah, f*** off!" Their next album, 1979's *Risqué*, produced an even bigger song, "Good Times." It was not only a massive hit, but was also sampled by hip-hop pioneers Grandmaster Flash and the Sugarhill Gang.

Chic were something of a victim of their own success. They became so synonymous with the all-conquering disco sound that they lost popularity when the backlash came. Still, Rodgers and Edwards worked successfully behind the scenes, producing records alone or together for artists such as David Bowie (see page 10), Debbie Harry (see page 9), Diana Ross, and Madonna.

The band reunited in the late '80s and released *Chic-Ism* in 1992. On tour in Japan in 1996, Edwards died of pneumonia, while Thompson died in 2003. Nile Rodgers has recently enjoyed a golden period, collaborating with Daft Punk (see page 100) on 2013's hit "Get Lucky." In 2018 he released *It's About Time*, the first Chic album in 24 years, partially based on tapes featuring Edwards and Thompson.

TOP ALBUM *Chic* (1977), despite its terrible cover. From the opening bars of Bernard Edward's bass, you're transported to a classy club in late '70s New York, where you're dancing with impossibly glamorous people.

POP TRIVIA Nile Rodgers and Bernard Edwards first met while playing in the touring band for the *Sesame Street* stage show. Rodgers took over from Carlos Alomar, who later became Bowie's dependable rhythm guitarist. Presumably, Rodgers was more Kermit-ed to the project.

ROXY MUSIC

In the early 1970s Roxy Music were glam rock competitors to David Bowie (see page 10). Like him they brought avant-garde tendencies to pop music and wore outrageous stage outfits. While Bowie embarked on his series of schizophrenic transformations, Bryan Ferry's troupe pursued a vision of glamorous sophistication.

Roxy Music's sound was partially the result of their unusual line-up. In addition to vocals, guitar, bass, and drums, the band featured Andy Mackay on saxophone and oboe, and self-professed "non-musician" Brian Eno on synthesizer, tape loops, and "treatments." On their first album, *Roxy Music* (1972), they shifted from seductive cabaret, through rock 'n' roll and pastiche-country, to sci-fi jazz, sometimes in the space of one song. Despite (or perhaps because of) this exuberant experimentalism, the album found an instant following in the UK, particularly after the band played surreal masterpiece "Virginia Plain" on the BBC's *Top of the Pops*. This single was not included on the original album, but is included on all re-issues.

They released another non-album single—the glorious "Pyjamarama"—to promote the album *For Your Pleasure* (1973). Eno left the band after considerable friction with Ferry over the leadership and direction of the band. Brian Eno (whose name is an anagram of Brain One) was arguably the group's mad professor, developing new sounds from maltreated bits of technology, and took something of this spirit with him when he left.

Over the next few albums, Ferry steered Roxy Music in a less experimental but sophisticated direction, creating a dark, crooning art-rock. Ferry became the louche Noel Coward of rock, speak-singing with his distinctive vibrato. This period culminated with 1975's *Siren*, featuring "Love is the Drug," the band's only US hit single. Chic's Nile Rodgers (see page 31) has said that the song's bass line was a direct influence on their song "Good Times."

Roxy Music returned in 1979 with Manifesto, whose shorter and more direct songs were seen as a reaction to punk and new wave. In truth, *Manifesto* drifts frequently into the realm of '80s MOR (middle of the road) rock. The band, who at this point comprised only Ferry, Mackay, guitarist Phil Manzanera, and various session musicians, continued this move toward smooth, anaemic balladry on *Flesh and Blood* (1980), which is a world away from their startling debut. Still, on their final record, *Avalon* (1982), this gentler approach finally came to fruition—the smooth soundscapes and subtle arrangements suit the ruminative, melancholic songs.

Ferry has made many solo albums and continues to record and perform. In interviews he now comes across as the Roger Moore or even Prince Charles of rock. Brian Eno, of course, went on to apply his massive, inquisitive brain to his own albums, as well as those of Bowie, Talking Heads (see page 34), Devo (see page 30), U2, and many others. He invented ambient music and composed the start-up music for Microsoft's Windows 95, which he later admitted to doing on a Mac.

TOP ALBUM *For Your Pleasure* (1973) Eno's still on board, so things are nice and weird, but it's a darker, more focused affair than the first album. Includes "In Every Dream Home a Heartache," a creepy paean to empty materialism (and love song to a blow-up doll), and the eerie, nine-minute oddity, "The Bogus Man." The album ends with weird effects, tape loops, and a fragmentary recording of Judi Dench.

POP TRIVIA Part of Roxy Music's glamorous image was the tradition of featuring scantily clad models on their record sleeves (Ferry was often dating them at the time). *Country Life* (1974) caused the band problems as its revealing photo of two German women was deemed obscene in some countries and covered up. In retrospect, putting a semi-naked model on the cover every time looks a bit icky and belies the sophistication of the material therein, but then I guess it was the '70s.

TALKING HEADS

Emerging from the CBGB's punk scene (seriously, they must have been putting something in the beer at CBGB), Talking Heads sounded even less punk than Blondie or Patti Smith.

The music was all jerky, clean-sounding guitars and soon headed for increasingly funky waters. David Byrne, by his own admission socially awkward, transformed his neuroses into yelps and strange dancing on stage and sang songs about cities, books, and life's minutiae.

Three members of the band—Byrne (vocals and guitar), Tina Weymouth (bass), and Chris Frantz (drums)—met at Rhode Island School of Design, and this art school background informed their restless experimentation. Recruiting additional guitarist and keyboard player Jerry Harrison, they released their first album *Talking Heads 77* in, erm, 1977. This album got some attention, not least because its popular single "Psycho Killer" came out a few months after the Son of Sam serial killings in New York.

The following album *More Songs About Buildings and Food* (1978) is in contention with Devo (see page 30) for best album title ever, and began a three-album association with producer Brian Eno (see page 32). It was Eno who pushed Talking Heads into more experimental areas, although ironically it was this album's cover of Al Green's "Take Me to the River" which brought them to a more mainstream audience.

Fear of Music (1979) had a darker, more paranoid tone than its predecessor, including references to contemporary political subjects. However, the band were also sounding their funkiest yet. They collaborated on one more album with Eno. 1980's *Remain in Light* (see right) is rhythmically complex and sonically dense, incorporating elements of funk, disco, and the influence of non-Western music, in particular Fela Kuti and afrobeat. Byrne and Eno would explore this terrain in more detail the following year in their non-Talking-Heads release, *My Life in the Bush of Ghosts*.

Speaking in Tongues (1983) produced the band's only Top 10 hit in the US, the none-more-funky "Burning Down the House." The following tour, with a bolstered line-up of musicians and backing singers, was captured by Jonathan Demme in his film *Stop Making Sense*. It's widely regarded as the best ever concert film and culminates in Byrne dancing on stage in a massive, oversized suit.

The following three albums produced more mainstream hits, including "Road to Nowhere," "Wild Wild Life," and "Radio Head" (from which the band took their name). After 1988's *Naked* the band drifted apart, with an acrimonious split between Byrne and the other members. Byrne has made numerous solo albums, started "world music" label Luaka Bop, written books on music and cycling, and collaborated with artists including St. Vincent (see page 150), Fatboy Slim, and Anna Calvi. His 2019 *American Utopia* concert tour received rave reviews. Weymouth and Frantz (who are married) started the offshoot band Tom Tom Club while still in Talking Heads, and have continued to record and occasionally tour.

TOP ALBUM *Remain in Light* (1980) The only thing wrong with this album is that everything else, by Talking Heads or anyone else, sounds so *ordinary* afterward. Byrne barks his gnomic utterances over skittish grooves. It sounds like a tribal past and digital future all at the same time. It also yielded one of the band's signature tunes, the midlife crisis monolog "Once in a Lifetime," which was helped into the public consciousness by a memorable video.

POP TRIVIA After David Byrne called time on Talking Heads, Weymouth, Frantz, and Harrison reunited for one more album under the name of The Heads. *No Talking, Just Head* (1996) featured guest vocalists, including Debbie Harry (see page 9), XTC's Andy Partridge (see page 65), and Shaun Ryder of the Happy Mondays. Byrne took legal action to prevent them using the name Talking Heads. Did I mention that they weren't really getting on by this point?

Parliament & FUNKADELIC

If George Clinton did not exist, it would be necessary to invent him. Under the banners of Parliament and Funkadelic he brought his appealingly wacky musical vision to the world, a delicious mixture of psychedelia, sci-fi, and squelchy funk.

For a band that ended up so weird, Parliament started out as a fairly conventional doo-wop band, The Parliaments. During a contractual dispute with his record label, Clinton was prevented from using The Parliament's name, so signed the band to a different label as Funkadelic. In 1970 he relaunched Parliament with more or less the same band members, meaning that he now had two bands with which to spread his increasingly cosmic vision of funk.

It's hard to tell where Parliament ends and Funkadelic starts. Notionally, Parliament was supposed to play more mainstream funk, based around vocals and horns, while Funkadelic showcased harder, guitar-based funk-rock, influenced by Hendrix and Sly Stone. In practice the two bands usually toured as Parliament-Funkadelic, a description that morphed into a name for the music itself, P-Funk. Clinton employed an ever-revolving cast of musicians, but important contributors who stuck around included top-hatted bass maestro Bootsy Collins and keyboard player Bernie Worrell (who also worked with Talking Heads, see page 34).

Clinton began working out an increasingly complicated mythology of P-Funk for both groups, drawing elements from Christianity, Sun Ra, and science fiction. Parliament's 1975 album *Mothership Connection* introduced the messianic alien, Starchild, who came to bring the Funk to mankind. He reappears on subsequent albums, along with Dr. Funkenstein and the repressive Sir Nose D'Voidoffunk, who wants to stop humanity from dancing. No, I have no idea either, but it's

great fun! Funkadelic albums tend to be less narrative, with more emphasis on an expansive, socially conscious mind-set. "Maggot Brain," described on the 1971 album of the same name, is an insular small-mindedness beyond which man must evolve to avoid global catastrophe.

Parliament-Funkadelic live was a riotous affair. The band(s) would perform in surreal costumes—to represent Starchild, for example, guitarist Garry Shider would perform wearing a nappy.

Clinton officially wound up Parliament and Funkadelic in the early 1980s, but many of his musicians continued to record and play together under his name or the P-Funk All Stars. Parliament released the brilliantly named *Medicaid Fraud Dog* in 2018 and Clinton announced his retirement from touring in 2019, suggesting that his place on stage would be taken by a hologram.

TOP ALBUM *Funkentelechy Vs. the Placebo Syndrome* (1977) Sir Nose D'Voidoffunk is on the loose, trying to infect humanity with the Placebo Syndrome. Thankfully, Starchild is at hand with his Bop Gun to restore the Funk. Funkentelechy will prevail! The original LP came with an eight-page comic book by Overton Loyd.

POP TRIVIA Though P-Funk fell out of favor in the electronic '80s, a new generation of fans has fallen under its spell, thanks to its extensive sampling in hip-hop. Parliament-Funkadelic have been sampled by acts including De La Soul (see page 62), Public Enemy (see page 68), Digital Underground, Ice Cube, and er... MC Hammer.

KRAFTWERK

It's only a slight exaggeration to say that Kraftwerk invented the 1980s. Listen to their pioneering electronic albums of the '70s and you can hear the seeds of house, techno, and hip-hop, as well as more mainstream dance music and synth-pop.

Kraftwerk (German for power station) was started by Ralf Hütter and Florian Schneider in Düsseldorf and grew out of the German experimental music scene of the time, jokingly dubbed "Krautrock" by UK music paper *Melody Maker*. Hütter and Schneider were influenced by a wide range of music, including folk, American rock (MC5 and The Stooges), and classical (Stockhausen).

Their first albums sound little like the repetitive, pulsating music of classic Kraftwerk. *Kraftwerk 1* (1970) and *Kraftwerk 2* (1972) are hippyish, freeform improvisations played on traditional instruments, including quite a lot of Schneider's flute. 1973's *Ralf und Florian* moved closer to the classic sound, including their first use of the vocoder, but it was *Autobahn* (1974) that cemented their style and reputation as electronic innovators. It also introduced the ongoing metaphors of technological progress and travel.

The international success of *Autobahn* meant that the band could tour more widely, reaching audiences in the US and the UK, as well as mainland Europe. Hütter and Schneider were joined by Wolfgang Flür and Karl Bartos to form what is now considered to be the classic line-up. Live, they sang through vocoders and played keyboard synthesizers and self-built drum machines.

They continued their literal and conceptual exploration of technology on 1975's *Radio-Activity* (see right) and returned to the concept of travel with 1977's *Trans-Europe Express*. The title song name-checked Iggy Pop (see page 18) and David Bowie (see page 10). Bowie had publicly acknowledged his stylistic debt to Kraftwerk, asking them to support him on tour (they declined) and paying a backhanded compliment in the title of "V-2 Schneider" from *Heroes* (1977).

On *The Man-Machine* (1978) they extended their technological obsession into the realms of artificial intelligence and automation, presenting themselves as robots. The highly stylized black and red cover, inspired by Russian Suprematist artist El Lissitzky, became the iconic image of the band, and one that has been spoofed ever since.

Their next album *Computer World* (1981) included some of their chilliest and most lovely melodies ("Computer Love" and "Computer World"), but it was "The Model" (originally a track from *The Man-Machine*, re-released as the B-side of "Computer World") which became a Number One hit in the UK. "The Model" is slight and accessible by Kraftwerk's standards, and also a relatively straightforward tale of male lust. In it, you can hear the blueprint of every synth band of the '80s, including Depeche Mode (see page 71) and the Human League.

To date, Kraftwerk have made two more albums of original material, 1986's *Electric Cafe* and 2003's *Tour de France Soundtracks* (released to coincide with the 100th anniversary of the sporting event, but confusingly based on their "Tour de France" single from 1983). Though Schneider left Kraftwerk in 2008, the group continued to perform with Hütter as the only original member. Florian Schneider's death was announced in May 2020.

TOP ALBUM *Radio-Activity* (1975) This opens with the ominous sound of a Geiger counter. The whole album is an ambiguous hymn to the possibilities of science and technology, including radioactive power, but also remote communication, hence the hyphen between "Radio" and "Activity." If you need any more evidence that there's a playful sense of humor beneath Kraftwerk's chilly mechanics, the album finishes with a song titled "Ohm Sweet Ohm."

POP TRIVIA Despite being famously reclusive, Kraftwerk became famous for their innovative performances, involving video projection and sequencing. On their 1981 tour, "The Robots" was famously "performed" by mannequins in place of the band. In 2013 they performed their "catalog", the eight albums from *Autobahn* to *Tour de France* over eight nights at London's Tate Modern (appropriately enough, this was originally a power station). The huge demand for tickets crashed the Tate's website.

WIRE

Latest in our list of punk bands who weren't really punk is Wire. Formed in London in 1976, Wire were inspired by punk, but their artsy sensibilities set them apart from the more rabble-rousing scene centered on the Sex Pistols.

Wire's often perverse, avant-garde tendencies have steered them in many strange directions over 14 albums and various spin-off and solo releases. While they have always been a fiercely loved cult act, their influence can be heard in a diverse range of bigger-selling bands, including R.E.M. (see page 72), Sonic Youth (see page 43), and Blur (see page 78).

Their debut album, *Pink Flag* (1977), is still considered their classic album. It undoubtedly speaks the newly coined vocabulary of punk (crunchy guitars, vocals spat in a distinctly London accent) but from the dissonant opening bars of "Reuters," it's clear we are in stranger terrain than the Pistols' amped up rock 'n' roll. Across the album's 21 songs, they experiment with song structures and lengths (six tracks come in under the one minute mark), mixing savage salvos of guitar with atonal drones and layered, shouting vocals.

The next two albums, *Chairs Missing* (1978) and *154* (1979), continued this experimental approach, dialing back the punk angst in favor of subtler, sinister soundscapes and pop melodies. Wire split in 1981, but reformed in 1985. Drummer Robert Grey left the band in 1990 and they rechristened themselves Wir before splitting up again until the late '90s.

Wire's music has gone through many stylistic changes. The current line-up includes three of the original members, Colin Newman, Graham Lewis, and Robert Grey, along with guitarist Matthew Simmons. Being 30 years younger than the rest of the band, Simmons looks like the long-haired Dorian Gray of the group. Wire have been impressively prolific in recent years, releasing four albums since 2015. Their latest, *Mind Hive*, is taut, angular and mellow by turns, with abstruse lyrics that hint at doom and savage violence.

TOP ALBUM *Chairs Missing* (1978) This further extends the stylistic range of *Pink Flag*, but invests its songs with more structure. The spiky guitars are present but are mingled with atmospheric synth parts, ominous echoes, and choral backing vocals. Includes deranged sing-a-long "I am the Fly" and the baffling, but beautiful, pop gem "Outdoor Miner."

POP TRIVIA In 1981, Wire posthumously released the live album *Document and Eyewitness*, a recording of performances from 1980 that combined unheard material and confrontational performance art intended to wind up a punk audience. Music journalist Mike Barnes describes this period as a "public act of commercial suicide."

THE SPECIALS

This was the sound of urban multiculturalism in the UK in the late 1970s, but crucially not of London. The Specials came from economically depressed Coventry, and their songs were full of references to unemployment, racism, teen pregnancy, and the hopelessness of youth in Thatcher's Britain.

The Specials struck a chord with the nation's youth and their rise was meteoric, culminating in the anthem of urban alienation, "Ghost Town," which spent three weeks at Number One during the English riots of 1981. They brought ska to a wider audience and were also notable for releasing their music independently through their own 2 Tone Records. Though lead singer Terry Hall became the best-known member of the group, The Specials were the brainchild of keyboard player Jerry Dammers, who wanted to create a ska-revival band, incorporating white and black band members, with an anti-racist message.

Their first album, *Specials* (1979), was produced by Elvis Costello (see page 25) and featured songs about racial conflict, urban violence, and youthful disillusionment with society. Their second album, *More Specials* (1980), headed away from their ska origins into stranger sounds, but by then it was too late. The band was riven with internal strife and most of the

members had lost faith in Dammers' musical vision. Not long after the success of "Ghost Town," Terry Hall, Neville Staple, and Lynval Golding broke away to form new wave pop group, Fun Boy Three. Dammers regrouped under the banner Special AKA, adding new musicians and singers to the remaining Specials and recorded one more album, *In the Studio*.

The Specials reformed without Dammers in 2009 and toured for the next few years. Drummer John Bradbury died in 2015. In 2019 The Specials, now just Terry Hall, Lynval Golding, and Horace Panter from the original band, released *Encore*, a new album that dabbled with disco and funk alongside their trademark ska.

TOP ALBUM *More Specials* (1980) This album is much more ambitious than the first. Dammers seems to be trying to create some kind of weird amalgam of dub, cocktail jazz, and Morricone mood-music. His eclectic vision alienated many members of the band, but it created some fantastic moments, including "Man at C&A," "Stereotype," and "International Jet Set," and pointed toward his sonic masterpiece, "Ghost Town."

POP TRIVIA For a time, Dammers had his own mini-Motown in the shape of 2 Tone Records, which put out music by The Specials and other ska acts such as The Beat, The Selecter, and Madness. 2 Tone benefited from great branding. Its famous "Walt Jabsco" logo, showing the classic rude boy in pork pie hat and loafers, was based on a photo of Peter Tosh of the Wailers.

CHAPTER TWO

THE Eighties STAGE

FEATURING THE FOLLOWING ARTISTS:

SONIC YOUTH
Kate Bush
THE SMITHS
The Fall
JOY DIVISION & NEW ORDER
SPINAL TAP
THE JESUS AND MARY CHAIN
THE CURE
DINOSAUR JR.
FUGAZI
Pixies

PRINCE
DE LA SOUL
RUN-D.M.C.
Cocteau Twins
XTC
BEASTIE BOYS
PUBLIC ENEMY
THE POGUES
DEPECHE MODE
R.E.M.

INDIE ★ HARDCORE ★ ELECTRO ★ SKA ★ HIP-HOP

SONIC YOUTH

Sonic Youth were perhaps the greatest noisy guitar band of the 1980s and '90s. Though they didn't stay youthful longer than anyone else, the "sonic" bit of their name could usually be relied upon to deliver.

The New York band was started in 1981 by Kim Gordon and Thurston Moore (who later married). Lee Ranaldo joined soon after and the three remained its musical core. They became known early on for their extreme "noise rock," with Moore and Ranaldo's cranked-up guitars tuned to weird intervals (an influence of Joni Mitchell, see page 12) and sometimes customized with objects jammed beneath the fret boards. Gordon and Moore became the poster couple for alternative music, with Kim deified as a rock goddess. Boys wanted to kiss her and girls wanted to be her, or sometimes the other way round.

In 1987 they released *Sister*, a loose concept album inspired by the life of troubled science fiction writer Philip K. Dick. Next came three of their biggest albums. *Daydream Nation* (1988) was a double album and the first recording to do justice to their extended improvisations. They showed their arty leanings by using a Gerhard Richter painting for the album's cover. *Goo* (1990) was their first album for major label Geffen and perhaps the most accessible record of their career. By 1992 America had caught up with bands like Sonic Youth and Dinosaur Jr. (see page 56), and there was a renewed interest in their music. Sonic Youth hired Butch Vig—who had recently produced Nirvana's *Nevermind* (see page 84)—to work on their next record *Dirty* (1992). "Youth Against Fascism" featured guest guitar from Fugazi's Ian MacKaye (see page 57), whose first band Minor Threat had been an early influence on their music.

During the '90s and into the new century, Sonic Youth continued releasing music, including a series of experimental instrumental albums on their own label, SYR. The band hit the skids in 2011, when Gordon and Moore announced that they were separating after 27 years of marriage. Gordon, Moore, and Ranaldo have all embarked on a bewildering range of projects since, including solo albums, new bands, soundtracks, and TV and film appearances.

TOP ALBUM *Goo* (1990) This album saw the band corralling their guitar skronks into more recognizably song-shaped structures and engaging with a new audience. It's still noisy and strange, though. In "Tunic (Song for Karen)," Gordon imagines Karen Carpenter in heaven, playing drums with Elvis and other deceased music stars. The album also includes the only Sonic Youth song you hear on the radio: the feminist anthem "Kool Thing," which has guest vocals from Public Enemy's Chuck D (see page 68). The cover features a drawing by artist and one-time member of Black Flag, Raymond Pettibon, and is based on a photo of the sister and brother-in-law of the Moors murderer, Myra Hindley, on their way to her trial.

POP TRIVIA In 2015, Harper Collins released Kim Gordon's autobiography, *Girl in a Band*, in which she writes frankly about her time in Sonic Youth, her marriage to Thurston Moore, and the reasons for their divorce. It's fair to say that some fans were a little less keen on Moore after reading it.

Kate Bush

My first memory of Kate Bush is of a friend bringing in a video of "Wuthering Heights" to our school English lesson, when we were studying the book. British television audiences encountered her in much the same way in the late 1970s, as the wide-eyed whirling dervish singing about Heathcliff and Cathy.

On television, Kate Bush's outfits and eccentric dancing captured attention. On record, her unique delivery did the same—the high-pitched yelps and cut-glass enunciation, or the soulful maturity that she brought to "The Man with the Child in his Eyes" from 1978's debut album *The Kick Inside*.

In the 80s, Bush was one of the most consistently interesting and experimental pop musicians around. She managed proper pop-star levels of fame, while following an idiosyncratic path, guided by her eccentric instincts and enthusiasms. She felt rushed by her record company into recording second album *Lionheart* (1980) and from then on exercised a determined control over her own career that was remarkable for her age and the era.

Never For Ever (1980) produced bonkers hit "Babooshka," which forced a nation's dads to spit out their tea when they saw *that* outfit on Top of the Pops. 1982's The Dreaming was the first album Bush produced herself and she took the opportunity to create complicated and dense musical textures. It included the mad gavotte of "Sat in Your Lap," while the title track, inspired by Australian Aboriginal culture, features some pretty dodgy Australian accents.

Bush's next album was her popular masterpiece *Hounds of Love* (1985), on which her increasingly sophisticated songwriting and production meshed perfectly with her pop sensibilities (see right).

On the follow-up album, *The Sensual World* (1989), she filtered a newly explicit sexuality with her literary interests, quoting from Molly Bloom's erotic conclusion to Joyce's *Ulysses*. Bush recorded one more typically diverse album, *The Red Shoes* (1993), before hanging up her hat (and leotard) for over a decade.

During this time she withdrew from showbiz and concentrated on family life, raising a son with her husband and guitarist Danny McIntosh. We finally heard the results of that creative project in 2005 when she released *Aerial*. The double-album featured a Renaissance-style ode to Bush's son, "Bertie," and on the second disc's song suite, "An Endless Sky of Honey," the boy himself contributed a spoken-word sample. He also sang the part of a snowflake on 2011's *50 Words for Snow*, which features contributions from Elton John and Stephen Fry.

TOP ALBUM *Hounds of Love* (1985) This is pretty much perfect. Side one includes four of her catchiest pop songs—"Running Up That Hill," "Hounds of Love" (which was later covered by Sunderland indie band The Futureheads), "The Big Sky," and "Cloudbusting"—but also manages to be completely mad. "Cloudbusting" is about maverick psychologist Wilhelm Reich, for God's sake. Side two is devoted to "The Ninth Wave," a suite of seven songs describing someone almost drowning in the ocean. She performed the whole of "The Ninth Wave" live in 2014 (see below).

POP TRIVIA For an artist whose creative appeal was so wrapped up in dance and physical performance, Bush was notable for her reluctance to perform live. She had made only very sporadic live appearances since her first and only tour in 1979. Fans were, therefore, happily stunned when in 2014 she announced a 22-date residency at London's Hammersmith Apollo. *Before the Dawn* featured lavish stage design, costume, and choreography, and was received and reviewed as a creative tour de force.

THE SMITHS

Perhaps more than any other band, The Smiths set the template for what a British indie band should be—a dynamic cult group on a hip label (but close enough to the mainstream to get on *Top of the Pops*), with a direct line to their loyal fans.

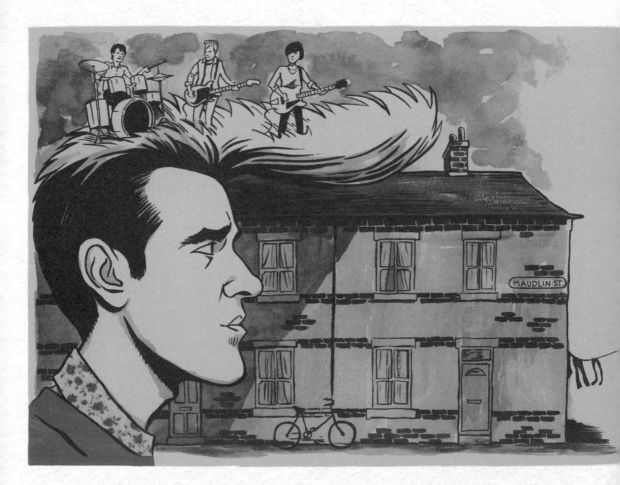

Johnny Marr was the founding force behind The Smiths and the band's musical leader. It was he who knocked on Morrissey's door and he who recruited Andy Rourke (bass) and Mike Joyce (drums) from Manchester's pool of amateur musicians. Rourke and Joyce were a great rhythm section (listen to "Barbarism Begins at Home" from *Meat is Murder*, 1985, for proof that The Smiths were a top-drawer funk band). But Marr wrote those melodies and embroidered the band's distinctive sound, combining the energy of punk with his shimmering guitar-playing, drawn from '60s bands like The Byrds.

The other side of The Smiths' appeal was Morrissey. Whereas later Manchester bands emphasized the city's hedonism and entrepreneurial, civic pride, Morrissey's Manchester was always a place of gloom, repressed sexual longing, cruelty, and even death (memories of the Moors Murders hang heavy over 1984's debut, *The Smiths*). Morrissey wasn't the first overtly poetic singer (see Patti Smith, page 28, or Leonard Cohen), nor was he the first Mancunian to sing about everyday romantic failure (see Buzzcocks, page 24), but in 1984 he was unlike anyone else, a captivating inversion of rock stereotypes. Bowie had been androgynous, but fierce and dominant. Morrissey was a self-taught bookworm who quoted Oscar Wilde, a card-carrying vegetarian, and an apparently celibate object of desire for his fans.

Morrissey was obsessed with kitchen-sink dramas from the 1950s and '60s, and used stills from such films in the band's artful, monochrome record sleeves. But his miserablist reputation obscures the playful wit of Morrissey's writing for The Smiths. His lyrics are melancholic and pessimistic, but peppered with hilarious non-sequiturs and withering put-downs.

Given the huge influence The Smiths have had on indie and alternative music, it's surprising how briefly they actually existed. From Marr knocking on that door to the posthumous release of their final album, *Strangeways, Here We Come* (1987), it was all over in five years. But in that short time they released four studio albums, including their acknowledged masterpiece *The Queen is Dead* (1986), and an unmatched run of brilliant singles.

The Smiths fell apart when the relationship between Morrissey and Marr soured. Morrissey embarked on a solo career, finding popularity in the US and a fanatical following in Latin America. His albums vary widely in quality, but on occasions have reached the heights of The Smiths—for example, on 1994's *Vauxhall and I*. Morrissey's once enlivening *bon mots* against the establishment have in recent years degenerated into self-pitying rants and troubling pronouncements on race and multiculturalism. Fans who had been inclined to give him the benefit of the doubt in earlier interviews were appalled when he expressed admiration for Nigel Farage and far-right political party For Britain.

Marr has lent his musical chops to various bands, including The Pretenders, and collaborated with New Order's Bernard Sumner (see page 50) in Electronic. Recently he has stepped forward as singer, releasing three albums under his own name.

TOP ALBUM *Hatful of Hollow* (1984) The Smiths were a prolific singles band who wrote B-sides that were as good as (sometimes better than) the A-sides. They also recorded versions of their songs for the BBC's John Peel that are better than those on their first album. This compilation album captures the excitement and quality of their early material, including "This Charming Man" and the extraordinary "How Soon is Now?".

POP TRIVIA These days, Morrissey has turned his acid quill to literature. His autobiography—entitled *Autobiography*—was published by Penguin in 2013. It's 450 pages long and contains some of the best and worst writing I have ever read, sometimes on the same page. In 2015, Penguin published his first novel, *List of the Lost*, about a '70s relay team. It received universally terrible reviews and won the Bad Sex Award, which is given to a book with the worst written sex scene. Marr's 2016 autobiography, *Set the Boy Free*, describes his time in The Smiths in notably sunnier prose than Morrissey's.

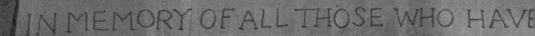

IN MEMORY OF ALL THOSE WHO HAVE

THE FALL

BRAMAH	ROGERS	OOKS
BAINES	WOLSTENC	HAM
FRIEL	SCHOFIE	AD
ORMROD	BUSH	DING
BURNS	NAGLE	LA
CARROLL		
RILEY		
PAWLETT		
LEIGH		
HANLEY		
SCANLON		
HANLEY		
SMITH		

RV'ED IN

ANEY
RTWISTLE
ITCHARD
ILNER
ATTS
CHER
RAFFORD
ESLEY
CCORD
OULOU
PURR
ENWAY
ELLING
JARRATT

The Fall

For decades you had to be careful drinking in the less salubrious pubs of Manchester. If you discovered a blackened coin at the bottom of your pint, you had been legally dragooned into The Fall for at least one album, or until Mark E. Smith got sick of you.

The grizzled Captain Ahab of alternative music, Smith led The Fall since its launch as a cerebral, experimental punk band in 1976. Since their debut album, the brilliantly titled *Live at the Witch Trials* (1979), they released 31 studio albums on at least 12 labels and countless live albums and compilations. DJ John Peel memorably said, "they are always different; they are always the same" and, over 40 years, their music constantly mutated under the direction of Smith and his ever-changing personnel. By the reckoning of Dave Simpson, author of *The Fallen: Life In and Out of Britain's Most Insane Group*, the band included between 40 and 60 members over the years (depending on where you draw the line between membership and collaboration). In truth, it's a notional "they" when talking about The Fall. The only constant in the band's history was Mark E. Smith and his bizarrely inflected vocals, full of rants, word play, verbal attacks, and oblique shaggy dog stories.

The Fall's back-catalog is so vast and confusing that it's best just to jump in, but here are a few suggested entry points. *Live at the Witch Trials* (1979) establishes the band's avant-garde, repetitive blueprint. *Hex Enduction Hour* (1982) is considered by many to be the group's best album. *This Nation's Saving Grace* (1985) is The Fall at their most accessible.

Smith's persona had been so pickled by years of substance and alcohol abuse that he had started to seem immortal, a grizzled Easter Island head of alternative music, but in 2018 he succumbed to the inevitable. It turned out he was mortal after all.

TOP ALBUM *I Am Kurious Oranj* (1988) Even by The Fall's standards, this is an odd album, but one that benefits from Brix Smith's ear for melody. The result of a collaboration with experimental ballet dancer and choreographer Michael Clark, it includes a reworking of Hubert Parry and William Blake's hymn "Jerusalem," in which Mark E. Smith equates Blake's vision of heaven on earth with his own demand that the council pay him compensation for slipping on a banana skin.

POP TRIVIA Mark E. Smith has said, "If it's me and your granny on bongos, then it's The Fall," but this proved not to be the case on at least one occasion. In 2004 he collaborated with German electronic music duo Mouse on Mars under the name Von Südenfed to produce *Tromatic Reflexxions*, which sounds like Smith shouting at some Germans in a nightclub.

JOY DIVISION & NEW ORDER

To start one influential, world-changing band may be good fortune; to start two begins to look like showing off.

Play Joy Division's *Unknown Pleasures* (1979) followed by, say, New Order's *Technique* (1989) and it's not immediately apparent that you're listening to more or less the same band. It's remarkable that Bernard Sumner, Peter Hook, and Stephen Morris survived the traumatic end of Joy Division, let alone went on to define the sound of the innovative '80s.

Those who find The Smiths "depressing" probably haven't heard Joy Division's records. Originally named Warsaw after Bowie's "Warszawa" (see page 10), they took their new name from groups of sex slaves in Nazi concentration camps. Their two albums, *Unknown Pleasures* (1979) and *Closer* (1980), are echoey cathedrals of doom. They sound like someone having a panic attack in an empty aircraft hangar.

Much of this stark, sonic atmosphere is down to Factory Records' maverick producer Martin Hannett, who shaped the band's recordings into his own chilly take on their sound (much to the band's annoyance at the time). But the words were, of course, written and sung by Ian Curtis. They are elliptical fragments of despair, meditations on corruption and fear, like Sylvia Plath poems put to music. Curtis suffered from depression, as well as severe epilepsy, and on the eve of their first tour of America he hanged himself at his home in Macclesfield. He was 23. The band's second album *Closer* and popular single "Love Will Tear Us Apart" were released in 1980, after Curtis' death.

The members of Joy Division had all agreed not to continue the band if anyone left. Renaming themselves New Order, they added Morris' girlfriend Gillian Gilbert on keyboards. Initially, the band recorded songs written with Curtis before his death (including "Ceremony") and, on their early recordings, struggled to escape the legacy and sound of the earlier band. Later on—influenced by New York clubs and the growth of club culture in Manchester—they pioneered a dance-pop style that combined synths, drum machines, and guitars. This approach got its first extended outing on 1983's *Power, Corruption & Lies*. They continued to mix the electronic and analog elements of their sound on *Low-Life* (1985), *Brotherhood* (1986), and fan-favorite *Technique* (1989). After the demise of Factory Records they released *Republic* in 1993, which included the hit single "Regret." Succumbing to

exhaustion and infighting, they dissolved for five years before reforming in 1998. They have since released four albums, including 2015's *Music Complete*. Peter Hook left New Order in 2007 and has been involved in legal tussles with the rest of the band since.

Joy Division have become icons of musical seriousness and integrity, with Curtis canonized as the ultimate tragic poet of rock, while New Order's innovative cross-fertilization of dance and rock has influenced countless musicians, including Primal Scream (see page 93), The Chemical Brothers (see page 98), and Daft Punk (see page 100).

TOP ALBUM *Technique* (1989) New Order kept up the old-school approach of releasing non-album songs as singles, meaning that some of their biggest songs, including "Blue Monday," "True Faith," and "Temptation" are only to be found on compilation albums. Still, for a studio album, let's choose 1989's *Technique*, which finds the band at their Balearic best. It opens with full-on dance banger "Fine Time," and even on its downbeat guitar songs Sumner sounds like he's being miserable in the Ibizan summer sun.

POP TRIVIA Joy Division and New Order were the flagship bands of Factory Records, run by Manchester's situationist music mogul, Tony Wilson. Factory's influence and lack of business nous are both legendary. New Order's single "Blue Monday" remains the best-selling 12" single of all time, but its original packaging was so expensive that Factory lost money on each copy sold. Wilson also ploughed much of the money made by New Order into Manchester's famous nightclub, The Hacienda. Wilson, who died in 2007, was memorably portrayed by Steve Coogan in the 2002 film *24 Hour Party People*, which told the story of Factory and the "Madchester" scene.

SPINAL TAP

In the 1980s, Spinal Tap earned themselves a permanent place in the pantheon of alternative rock as one of England's loudest, and most punctual, bands.

The nucleus of the band, musical prodigies David St. Hubbins (vocals, guitar) and Nigel Tufnel (guitar, vocals), met at school in London and later played in skiffle and beat groups, including the Likely Lads, The Originals, and The New Originals. Joining with bass player Derek Smalls to form Spinal Tap, the band initially pursued a hippyish, flower-power direction before switching to heavier rock.

In the 1970s and '80s they became known for the innovations they brought to heavy metal. Like Kraftwerk (see page 38), they were technological visionaries. Tufnel's customized amps enabled him to outperform metal bands such as Black Sabbath (see page 14) by playing one louder, and he also experimented with alternative tunings in his violin-on-guitar solos. Simultaneously, St. Hubbins was bringing ever-greater lyrical sophistication to his songwriting—for example, on pastoral rocker "Sex Farm." Smalls' study of American music history and forgotten time signatures led to his musical masterpiece, "Jazz Odyssey."

The band gained a reputation for elaborate (yet reliable) stage sets and fabulous costumes. Roxy Music (see page 32) were fans of their look and they probably influenced the young Kate Bush's love of lycra (see page 44). However, Spinal Tap also received its fair share of adversity. At the time of writing, 18 drummers have died while playing with the band in a wide range of circumstances. In addition, during the early '80s, the band experienced a freak "selectivization" of their appeal, which forced them to play smaller venues. Their 1982 *Smell the Glove* tour was recorded for posterity in Marti Di Bergi's seminal documentary *This is Spinal Tap* (1984).

TOP ALBUM *Smell the Glove* (1984) The most prized record in my collection is undoubtedly Spinal Tap's masterpiece *Smell the Glove*. I say masterpiece, but I'm not honestly sure what songs are on there, as I've never unwrapped it. Just look at that cover! Smooth, jet-black, so black you can see yourself in both sides. No, don't touch it, don't even look at it—you've seen enough of that.

POP TRIVIA Though the band continues to play sporadically, Tufnel has also become a respected (if controversial) expert on the history of Stonehenge. Fans are still waiting for news on St. Hubbins' long-anticipated Jack the Ripper musical, *Saucy Jack*.

THE JESUS AND MARY CHAIN

The Jesus and Mary Chain wrote gorgeous melodies in the spirit of the Beach Boys, then drenched them in fuzz and feedback. In the process they became an iconic UK indie band.

Brothers Jim and William Reid formed the band in East Kilbride, Scotland, in the early 1980s, influenced by The Shangri-las and Phil Spector, but also The Velvet Underground (see page 16) and The Stooges (see page 18). Early gigs were legendarily chaotic affairs, with lead singer Jim Reid verbally (and on occasion physically) attacking the audience. The band embraced a literally stripped-back approach. Drummer Murray Dalgleish played only two drums and Douglas Hart had only two strings on his bass guitar, telling journalists "two is enough."

The band released their debut album *Psychocandy* in 1985 and its swooning melodies, rock 'n' roll attitude, and squalling guitars brought it instant cult acclaim. They courted controversy in the same year by releasing the single "Some Candy Talking." DJ Mike Smith sniffed out that the song might not actually be about a trip to the candy store and the song was banned from BBC Radio 1.

Follow-up album, *Darklands* (1987), was less abrasive than the debut album, making the band's debt to classic American rock and pop more explicit. The Reid brothers played almost every instrument on the record, replacing their string of drummers with drum machines. 1989's *Automatic* continued in this direction, with synth-bass and keyboards edging them closer to the sound of electro-punk duo Suicide. "Reverence" from 1992's *Honey's Dead* got them banned from Radio 1 again, with its death-wish references to Christ and JFK.

They recorded two more albums, *Stoned & Dethroned* (1994) and *Munki* (1998), before splitting up. They reformed in 2007 and have toured extensively since. In 2017, they released the long awaited album *Damage and Joy*.

TOP ALBUM *Psychocandy* (1985) is an indie-rock classic. The opening drum beat of "Just Like Honey" tips the hat to The Ronette's "Be My Baby" and from then on it's 39 minutes of woozy vocals and fuzzed-out guitars, redefining Phil Spector's wall of sound in the age of the effects pedal.

POP TRIVIA An early line-up of the band included Bobbie Gillespie, later of Primal Scream (see page 93) on drums. He was a school friend of indie-rock enabler and mischief-maker Alan McGee and the band were one of the first signings to his legendary label, Creation Records. Later on, the band recruited John Moore, who would go on to form middle-England concept band Black Box Recorder with Luke Haines.

THE CURE

The Cure are the band who sold a million cans of hairspray and persuaded boys it was OK to wear lipstick. They formed at school in Crawley, southern England, and went on to become one of the biggest alternative acts of the 1980s.

An ever-changing line-up has revolved around wild-haired, sad-eyed frontman Robert Smith, the only constant member of the group. The band's sound evolved from the brittle post-punk of their debut *Three Imaginary Boys* (1979) into the epic miserablism that helped to define the burgeoning Goth scene and reached its peak (or gloomy depths, depending on how you see it) in the 1982 album *Pornography*.

In the public imagination The Cure have long been summed up by the image of pale boys in black jumpers, mumbling suicidal lyrics (and not without reason), but Robert Smith also has a way with a goofy pop song and indulged this side of his songwriting on more upbeat albums, such as *The Head on the Door* (1985), and the indie disco stalwart "The Love Cats."

This oscillation between catchy, adorable pop and anguished dirge is part of the charm of The Cure. 1989's career highlight *Disintegration* leans more toward the somber side of things, but also contains the lush romance of "Lovesong" and the comically spooky "Lullaby" (check out the arachnophobic video, which manages to be silly and scary all at once). Robert Smith penned the most unashamedly joyous song of his career in 1992's "Friday I'm In Love" and the end of the working week was marginally improved forever. The band continues to tour and release material intermittently and an older, plumper Smith still manages to rock that iconic haircut. In 2018 they staged a huge 40th anniversary concert in London's Hyde Park and Smith curated Meltdown Festival.

TOP ALBUM *Wish* (1992) This is a fully realized demonstration of the band's emotional and stylistic repertoire. It skips between symphonic dirges ("Open" and "End"), open-veined laments ("Apart" and "Trust"), sassy seduction ("Wendy Time"), and shimmering, up-beat pop songs ("Doing the Unstuck" and "Friday I'm in Love"), but somehow hangs together as an album. Justly, it was the biggest-selling record of their career.

POP TRIVIA The band's first single, "Killing an Arab," caused controversy because some interpreted its title as racist. It was, in fact, an artful reference to Camus' famous novel *L'Etranger*, whose philosophically apathetic protagonist shoots an Arab man in French Algiers. In retrospect this was a sign of the existentialist angst that Smith would pursue in his lyrics.

MONDAY

TUESDAY, WEDNESDAY

THURSDAY

FRIDAY!

REPEAT...

DINOSAUR JR.

Dinosaur Jr. were the kings of slacker rock, characterized by J Mascis' drawling vocals and eviscerating guitar solos.

The music of Dinosaur Jr. somehow managed to sound aggressive and mellow at the same time. This was partially the result of their influences. Mascis, bassist Lou Barlow, and drummer Murph grew up playing in hardcore punk bands, but they were also fans of Neil Young (see page 27) and Black Sabbath (see page 14). Mascis has described the sound of the band as "ear-bleeding country." Mascis wrote all the songs on their debut album, *Dinosaur* (1985), but Barlow sang the majority of the lead vocals. On follow-up album, *You're Living All Over Me* (1987), Mascis took most of the vocals and began to exert more control over the band's sound. Their next album, *Bug* (1988), was something of a breakthrough in the UK, producing the indie hit "Freak Scene." Despite their increasing popularity, tensions in the band came to a head and Mascis fired Barlow from the band.

Dinosaur Jr.'s next album *Green Mind* (1991) was a J Mascis solo album in all but name. In addition to guitar, bass, and vocals, he recorded most of the drum parts. As grunge took off in the early 1990s, the band toured extensively, recruiting Mike Johnson to play bass. They recorded *Where You Been* (1993) as an actual band, with Johnson on bass and Murph playing most of the drum parts. This was their best-selling album and featured the single "Start Choppin." After touring the album, Murph quit the band. J Mascis recorded two more albums under the name Dinosaur Jr., but reverted to recording the vast majority himself. In 2000, he abandoned the name and started recording as J Mascis + The Fog.

In 2005, the original line-up of Mascis, Barlow, and Murph reformed. They have since released four albums, most recently 2016's *Give a Glimpse of What Yer Not*. The band was a big influence on grunge bands such as Nirvana (see page 84) and Pavement (see page 91), as well as Blur's Graham Coxon (see page 78).

TOP ALBUM *Bug* (1988) This captures the sound of early Dinosaur Jr., audibly still three guys playing together, but coalescing under Mascis' exacting musical direction. His songwriting finds a sweet spot between melody and atonal noise, although the latter definitely wins out on "Don't," on which Barlow screams, "Why don't you like me?" over and over again, from beneath a barrage of squealing guitars. We do, Lou, we really do.

POP TRIVIA The band were originally called Dinosaur, but were forced to add the distinguishing "Jr." by psychedelic-rock supergroup The Dinosaurs.

FUGAZI

By the time he started Fugazi, Ian MacKaye was already a key figure in hardcore punk, a veteran of Minor Threat, and accidental inventor of the "straight edge" subculture. Fugazi extended the musical range of hardcore, exploring new influences such as dub and funk. As MacKaye later said, he wanted a band "like The Stooges with reggae."

Minor Threat's famously ethical approach also carried over into Fugazi. They released all their own records on MacKaye's Dischord label, and did almost no promotion, instead forging a reputation through extensive tours and word of mouth. After alternative rock became mainstream in the early 1990s, they were offered record deals by major labels, but turned them all down. They also had a policy of keeping ticket prices as low as possible.

Fugazi's best-known song is "Waiting Room" from their first EP (and later collected on 1989's *13 Songs*). Early recordings featured Guy Picciotto as vocal "foil" to MacKaye's main vocals, a set-up inspired by hip-hop records, but Picciotto began contributing guitar with their first album *Repeater*

(1990). They recorded two more albums, *Steady Diet of Nothing* (1991) and *In on the Kill Taker* (1993), mixing frantic punk rock with dub and even jazzy elements. From *Red Medicine* (1995) onward they morphed into a full-blown "art-punk" band, throwing out oblique lyrical observations and building angular soundscapes that culminated in 2001's *The Argument*. In this they resembled UK art-punks Wire (see page 40), whose punkiest moment "12XU" MacKaye had covered in Minor Threat. Technically, Fugazi never split up but went on "indefinite hiatus" in 2003.

TOP ALBUM *Repeater* (1990) The band's ethical stance wasn't only reflected in their business practices, but also in their lyrics. "Merchandise" and "Blueprint" are scathing attacks on consumer society and artists who sell out. Sonically, their first studio album is riff-heavy hard rock, but with added dub and funk influences, and even hints of highlife guitar on the title track. Despite its complete lack of marketing or promotion, *Repeater* has sold over 2 million copies worldwide.

POP TRIVIA Fugazi were a famously hard-touring band, playing over 1,000 gigs between 1987 and 2003. I guess this makes them the opposite of slacker rock. Since 2011 the band has released recordings of 750 of these concerts through their website, which are available to download for a small fee.

Pixies

The Pixies were, and are, a fabulously odd band. They sounded like no one else and looked nothing like a rock band was supposed to: lead singer (and screamer) Black Francis, a tubby manchild in plaid, flanked by baby-faced guitar-genius Joey Santiago and bass player Kim Deal (seemingly oblivious to her own aura of effortless cool), and backed by lanky drummer David Lovering.

Though they achieved cult popularity in the UK and Europe, the Pixies were neglected in their native USA and serious success eluded them. However, their music outlasted them, becoming a massive influence on grunge and alternative rock bands such as Radiohead (see page 94). Kurt Cobain famously admitted that "Smells Like Teen Spirit" was his attempt at writing a Pixies' song. The Pixies' favorite trick of big dynamic contrasts (quiet verses, then hit the overdrive pedal on the choruses) was aped to the point of cliché.

But there's more to the Pixies' sound than the loud-quiet-loud trick. Their original run of albums, from 1987's *Come On Pilgrim* to 1991's *Trompe Le Monde*, is restlessly inventive, full of weird guitar hooks, strangled yelps, and sassy bass runs. I got into the Pixies at the same time as I got into Burt Bacharach and, strange as it sounds, they've always struck me as kindred spirits. Both play around with unusual time signatures, but the songs are so well crafted that it doesn't sound like they're doing it just to be clever.

Then there are Black Francis' winningly strange lyrics. His lyrical obsessions take in sexual jealousy, Old Testament violence, Greek myth, incest, and aliens. In the early songs, he sings in manic, splenetic bursts, punctuated by screams and occasional snatches of Spanish. You'd never guess he was from Boston!

Relationships in the band declined over their six-year career, in particular that of Black Francis and Kim Deal, and the band finally split in 1993. Black Francis renamed himself Frank Black (his real name is Charles Michael Kittridge Thompson IV) and embarked on a solo career. Kim Deal made albums with her other band The Breeders, including the Platinum-selling *Last Splash* (1993).

In 2004 the Pixies reformed and toured the US, Europe, and Japan. They continued touring over the next decade and after much "Will they? Won't they?" speculation, they started releasing new tracks in 2013, compiled on the album *Indie Cindy* in 2014. Kim Deal left the band in 2013 and was eventually replaced on bass by Paz Lenchantin. The band have since released two albums, *Head Carrier* (2016) and *Beneath the Eyrie* (2019).

The 2006 documentary *loudQUIETloud* follows the reformed Pixies on their 2004 tour and shows four people pathologically unable to communicate with each other. They appear so dysfunctional that it's a miracle they managed to create anything in the first place!

TOP ALBUMS *Come On Pilgrim* (1987), a mini album, and *Surfer Rosa* (1988) were released in quick succession and later sold as a "twofer." Between them they encapsulate the early Pixies sound of searing rock, menacing skiffle, deranged shrieking, and coolly intoned backing vocals, by turns scary, thrilling, and sexy. They still sound like nothing else on earth.

Trompe Le Monde (1992) This is one of the great "final albums," full of tantalizing sonic hints about where they might have headed next, had they not been so thoroughly sick of each other. It includes a song about the architect of the Eiffel Tower and the saddest song you'll ever hear about a holidaying alien, "Motorway to Roswell."

POP TRIVIA After the Pixies split up, Joey Santiago began composing music for films and documentaries. But the prize for best second career must go to drummer David Lovering who reinvented himself as educational magician The Scientific Phenomenalist.

"Debaser," from 1989 album *Doolittle*, references Luis Buñuel and Salvador Dali's short film *Un Chien Andalou*. The film contains two of the most infamous images of surrealist cinema: a woman's eyeball being sliced open with a razor blade and ants streaming from a wound in a man's hand.

PRINCE

To paraphrase Philip Larkin, Prince invented sex (and possibly the color purple) in 1983. He was one of the biggest (perhaps *the* biggest?) pop stars of the 1980s, but beneath the purple pomp and eccentricity was an innately talented musician, whose influence extends far beyond the realm of mainstream pop.

In fact, Prince had been banging on about sex since at least 1980. Though his 1978 debut *To You* featured a song called "Soft and Wet," his first two albums were largely soft, romantic affairs. The real filth began with 1980's appropriately titled *Dirty Mind*, whose explicit lyrics were matched by a musical turnaround, featuring clipped, electronic funk. Prince didn't *just* write about sex. "1999," from the 1982 album of the same name, is a classic use of pop misdirection, presenting the terrifying subject of nuclear annihilation as a catchy, upbeat dance number.

1999 was Prince's mainstream breakthrough, but the album and film *Purple Rain* (1984) conferred megastar status on him. The album was recorded with his backing band, the Revolution, and has sold over 22 million copies. During the '80s, Prince wrote and produced many albums for himself and others, varying widely in tone and style. His own music took in baroque pop ("Raspberry Beret"), neo-psychedelia ("Paisley Park"), minimalist funk ("Kiss"), and pseudo-spiritual rock-rap ("Alphabet Street").

In the '90s he became known for his eccentricities as much as his music. After the disappointing sales of his *Love Symbol* album, bearing only his newly minted personal symbol on the cover, he spectacularly fell out with his record company, Warner Bros. He changed his name to the same symbol and became known in the media as "the artist formerly known as Prince." Around this time he appeared on the BBC's *Top of the Pops* with "slave" written on his cheek. The following week, Blur's Dave Rowntree (see page 78) appeared with "Dave" written on his. Never one to labor a point, after finally parting

ways with Warner Bros., Prince released a 36-song, triple album called *Emancipation* (1996).

The 2010s were something of a renaissance for Prince. In 2014 he released two albums, *Plectrumelectrum* (with new band 3rdeyegirl) and *Art Official Age*, and embarked on a seemingly ad hoc tour of the UK, playing the first gig in the living room of Lianne La Havas. Still effortlessly prolific, he released two more albums, initially via Jay Z's Tidal streaming service, in 2015. This made it all the more surreal and tragic when Prince's death was reported on April 21, 2016. Though the circumstances remain unclear, it appears that Prince died of an accidental overdose of fentanyl. He was only 57, a tragically young age for such a talent to be taken from us.

TOP ALBUM *Sign o' the Times* (1987) Warner Bros. argued Prince down from a triple to a double album on this one, but it's still his most stylistically diverse record, combining rock, pop, soul, and funk with daringly minimalist arrangements. Lyrically too, it's varied and adventurous. The title track is a despairing, channel-hopping survey of the contemporary world, while "If I Was Your Girlfriend" is a gender-bending exploration of female intimacy.

POP TRIVIA Prince's potty-mouth was indirectly responsible for those Parental Advisory stickers you get on albums. In 1985, Tipper Gore (wife of politician and later Vice President, Al) heard her 11-year old daughter listening to "Dear Nikki" from *Purple Rain*. In response she co-founded the Parents Music Resource Center, which campaigned for the labeling of explicit material.

DE LA SOUL

In the late 1980s and early '90s, De La Soul were the joyful antidote to the grim, misogynistic tropes of gangsta rap. They sampled with kleptomaniac joy and rapped with consummate ease and offbeat wit.

De La Soul consists of Posdnuos, Dave, and Maseo. In the early days, Dave was more commonly known as Trugoy the Dove. "Trugoy," which is "yogurt" spelt backward, came from his love of yogurt. I love De La Soul just for that. Their debut album, *3 Feet High and Rising* (1989), was produced by Prince Paul, and was a commercial and critical success. Its comedy skits and positive lyrics established the group as a progressive hip-hop act at odds with the increasingly violent image of mainstream rap. The band summed up their upbeat message of peace and harmony in the concept of the "D.A.I.S.Y. Age," an acronym of "da inner sound, y'all," which was echoed in the cartoony, floral album artwork.

They rebelled against this neo-hippy image on their second album, *De La Soul is Dead* (1991), which showed a smashed pot with three drooping daisies on the front. But, if anything, this album was more explicitly critical of the violent, reductive nature of contemporary hip-hop. Not that they lost their wacky sense of humor. An ongoing skit is threaded through the album, in which some thugs discover De La Soul's new

tape and criticize it as they listen, pronouncing at its conclusion: "De La Soul is dead."

De La Soul have continued to release albums and mix-tapes since, including Posdnuos and Dave's meta-concept album *Plug 1 & Plug 2 Present... First Serve* (2012). In 2016, they released their Kickstarter-funded album *And the Anonymous Nobody*, the first full-length album featuring all three members in over a decade.

TOP ALBUM   3 Feet High and Rising (1989) I could be clever and pick a more obscure record but, really, why try to be cool when you can have this much fun? Their definitive album is a hyperactive hoot, like spending an hour with three good-natured kids with ADHD. They interrupt their own songs with comedy skits and sound-collage blizzards of samples. Then, every now and again, it all coalesces into a classic hip-pop moment, "The Magic Number," "Eye Know," or "Me, Myself and I."

POP TRIVIA   De La Soul have collaborated three times with Damon Albarn's Gorillaz (see page 78), firstly on 2005's "Feel Good Inc.", then on 2010's "Superfast Jellyfish" along with Gruff Rhys from the Super Furry Animals (see page 105) and most recently on "Momentz" from the 2017 album *Humanz*.

RUN-D.M.C.

Run-D.M.C. were one of the first big-selling hip-hop acts. Their sparse, punchy style established the sound of much 1980s rap music and their look was similarly influential, moving hip-hop's sartorial style away from the glam look of early rappers and toward street style with their trademark Adidas.

The group was formed by Joseph "Run" Simmons and Darryl "D.M.C." McDaniels in Queens, New York, in 1981, adding DJ Jam Master Jay to the line-up soon after. They were named Run-D.M.C. (initially to their displeasure) by Simmons' older brother, hip-hop entrepreneur Russell Simmons (co-founder of Def Jam Records). Their eponymous debut album, released in 1984, had an immediate impact. Whereas earlier hip-hop tended toward a laid-back, funky sound, Run-D.M.C. pioneered a harsher, staccato style, rapping together over sparse backing tracks. "It's Like That" sounds more like Kraftwerk (see page 38) than "Rapper's Delight," its robotic drum machine punctuated by stabs of synth. This more dissonant, in-your-face version of hip-hop would become a big influence on Public Enemy (see page 68).

On "Rock Box," Run-D.M.C. added rock guitar to the mix, creating a rap/rock crossover sound that the band would regularly return to and which paved the way for acts such as the Beastie Boys (see page 66) and Rage Against the Machine.

They pursued this rap/rock fusion on follow-up album *King of Rock* (1985) and the huge-selling *Raising Hell* (1986), featuring the mega-hit "Walk This Way," on which they collaborated with Aerosmith.

They released four more albums between 1988 and 2001, but their later years were dogged by an increasing musical and personal rift between Simmons and McDaniels. In 2002, Jam Master Jay was killed at his recording studio in Queens—the murder remains unsolved.

TOP ALBUM *Raising Hell* (1986) Sometimes a band hits an inspired point where the songs just pour out of them. Produced by Def Jam's *other* founder, Rick Rubin, *Raising Hell* captures Run-D.M.C. at the peak of their powers, not only jamming with rockers Aerosmith, but also waxing lyrical on "Peter Piper" and rap anthems "It's Tricky," "My Adidas," and "You Be Illin'."

POP TRIVIA Both Simmons and McDaniels have had stints on TV since the band finished. Simmons (who has become a Pentecostal minister and now goes by the name of Rev Run) appeared with his family in reality TV series, *Run's House*. McDaniels, who had discovered he was adopted, filmed *DMC: My Adoption Journey*, in which he was reunited with his birth mother. He has since moved into the world of comics, writing himself as a hip-hop superhero in the comic book *DMC* for his own imprint Darryl Makes Comics.

Cocteau Twins

The Cocteau Twins created shimmering, moody dream-pop and were especially renowned for Elizabeth Fraser's unearthly voice. At times she would sing in an improvised, made-up "language," a technique that looked forward to Sigur Rós and back to Bowie's experiments on Low.

Formed by guitarist Robin Guthrie and bassist Will Heggie in Grangemouth, Scotland, the Cocteau Twins' early material, such as 1982's debut album *Garlands*, owed much to Goth and post-punk bands like Siouxsie and the Banshees and Bauhaus, as well as to Kate Bush (see page 44). Guthrie would layer recordings of his effects-heavy guitar to create their distinctive sound. Heggie left the band after their second EP, *Peppermint Pig*, while Fraser and Guthrie (who had become a couple) recorded their next album *Head Over Heels* as a duo.

The band recruited bass player and multi-instrumentalist Simon Raymonde and, over a series of EPs and third album *Treasure*, their sound blossomed into its full-blown, ethereal majesty. They released their most commercially successful album, *Heaven or Las Vegas*, in 1990 (see below), before parting ways with long-standing record label 4AD. In later years, the band began to falter under the strain of internal problems, in particular Guthrie's dependency on alcohol and drugs. Fraser and Guthrie separated in 1993 but worked together until the band split in 1997.

TOP ALBUM *Heaven or Las Vegas* (1990) All was not well while recording this album. Fraser had recently given birth to her and Guthrie's daughter, but he was mired in substance abuse. Raymonde was mourning his father's death. Not that you would know any of this from this kaleidoscopic and frequently joyful masterpiece. They channeled their emotional upheavals into songs whose expansive beauty belies their brevity. It includes some of their finest moments: "Iceblink Luck" and the title track.

POP TRIVIA For most of their career, the Twins were signed to record label 4AD, but Raymonde and Guthrie set up their own label Bella Union in 1997. Now run by Raymonde, it's one of the most respected independent labels around, with acts on the roster including Fleet Foxes (see page 126) and The Flaming Lips (see page 108).

XTC

Are XTC the most underrated band of the 1980s? Between 1978 and 1992 they made 10 adventurous albums of crafted guitar pop that ran the gamut from spiky new wave to psychedelia.

One thing that hobbled XTC's popularity was lead singer Andy Partridge's decision to withdraw from live performance after a debilitating bout of stage fright in 1982. Like The Beatles—but without as many screaming fans—they became a studio band, concentrating on their increasingly sophisticated album releases.

XTC started as a jerky, hyperactive new wave band, with twin songwriters Andy Partridge (vocals, guitar) and Colin Moulding (vocals, bass). In addition to their self-penned compositions, debut album *White Music* (1978) included a dub-inflected cover of "All Along the Watchtower." Partridge was the more prolific songwriter and typically provided two-thirds of the songs and vocals on an XTC album. However, it was Moulding who wrote and sang their breakthrough single from 1979's *Drums and Wires*, "Making Plans for Nigel." Over subsequent albums, they moved further away from punk and into more sophisticated songwriting that mixed '60s classic rock, US power pop, folk, and jazzier influences such as Steely Dan. Partridge's material, in particular, presents an acerbic, pessimistic take on the world, dressed in sunnier melodies. In 1986 the band traveled to Woodstock to record *Skylarking* with Todd Rundgren, in what should have been a perfect mesh of musical sensibilities. The sessions were legendarily fraught, with Partridge frequently clashing with the similarly wilful Rundgren. The band were unhappy with the result at the time, although *Skylarking* is now regarded as one of their best albums.

In 1992 they recorded *Nonsuch*, named after Henry VIII's palace, before going "on strike" in protest at the perceived mismanagement of their record label. Virgin finally terminated their contract in 1998, and they recorded two more albums, *Apple Venus Volume 1* (1999) and *Wasp Star (Apple Venus Volume 2)*, which emphasized their orchestral and guitar-heavy work, respectively. The band released these albums themselves, so they are consequently a little harder to get hold of.

TOP ALBUM *The Big Express* (1984) This finds XTC mid-way between the manic abandon of their early songs and the baroque arrangements of their later material. We are firmly in the landscape of pop, but what a varied and inventive take on pop it is. Moulding's "Wake Up" sounds like new wave played by robots, while Partridge's "Seagulls Screaming Kiss Her Kiss Her" is the sound of regret and paranoia played on a Bontempi organ. "The Everyday Story of Smalltown" is the missing link between The Kinks' observational miniatures and Blur (see page 78), while "This World Over" imagines the survivors of nuclear apocalypse looking back in regret, over a smooth, reggae-funk backing.

POP TRIVIA The band's fondness for '60s psychedelia spilled over into the songs of their alter egos, the Dukes of Stratosphear. The Dukes released two albums of cod-psychedelic rock, *25 O'Clock* (1985) and *Psonic Psunspot* (1987), which were compiled on the album *Chips from the Chocolate Fireball*.

BEASTIE BOYS

Together Ad Rock, Mike D, and MCA were the Beastie Boys. They were one of the most inventive, and perhaps the best-loved, hip-hop groups of the 1980s and '90s.

Undoubtedly, one of the reasons for the Beastie Boys' early popularity was that they reflected their fans: a crossover audience of white college kids. The Beasties became highly respected by other rap acts, including Run-D.M.C. (see page 63) and Q-Tip, but they were white, middle-class Jewish kids who fell in love with a predominantly black art form. The band started out as a hardcore punk band in New York, but soon switched to hip-hop, recording with Rick Rubin, the co-founder of new rap label Def Jam.

Their first album, *Licensed to Ill* (1986), was heavily influenced by Run-D.M.C., both in its rapping style and rock-guitar backing tracks. It featured the monster hits "(You Gotta) Fight for Your Right (To Party)" and "No Sleep Till Brooklyn." At this point, the band's image was of obnoxious frat boys who only wanted to get drunk and laid. The *Licensed to Ill* tour featured a huge inflatable penis and women dancing in cages.

The Beastie Boys retained their mischievous sense of humor and taste for the absurd, but left behind such macho posturing. Over time, they became one of the most progressive acts in hip-hop, apologizing for early homophobic slurs and, on the track "Sure Shot," calling for respect for women. In this, and in their evolving musical style, the group they most resembled was De La Soul (see page 62). *Paul's Boutique* (1988), produced by the Dust Brothers, was a massive step forward. It featured a bewildering array of samples from songs, movies, and commercials, layered and stitched together, while the three MCs rapped around and across each other with a newly found dexterity. *Paul's Boutique* was considered a commercial flop at the time, but is now regarded as a classic.

On *Check Your Head* (1992) the band picked up their instruments for the first time since their punk days and from then on they frequently combined live recordings with samples and beats. 1994's *Ill Communication* cemented their place as the favorite rap group of the grunge generation, not least because of the colossal "Sabotage," which was supported on MTV by a hilarious Spike Jonze video. Their next album, *Hello Nasty* (1998), was a 22-song, kaleidoscopic epic that mixed songs with rap tracks, and included sci-fi banger "Intergalactic." Its penultimate track, "Dr. Lee, PhD," featured legendary dub producer Lee "Scratch" Perry waxing lyrical over a wonky, reggae backing track.

In 2004, they returned to a more stripped-back, hip-hop sound on *To the 5 Boroughs*. In the wake of the 9/11 attack and the Iraq War, the album preached a message of harmony and engagement, but also had plenty of anger for the Bush government. They released two more records, instrumental *The Mix-Up* in 2007 and final rap album *Hot Sauce Committee Part Two* in 2011. The band was cut short by the tragic death of MCA (Adam Yauch) from cancer in 2012. Yauch, a practicing Buddhist, had been an active campaigner for Tibetan independence, organizing the Tibetan Freedom Concerts of the late 1990s and early 2000s. Out of respect for their friend, Mike D and Ad Rock have decided not to continue the Beastie Boys. In 2018, Mike D and Ad Rock released the *Beastie Boys Book*, a 500-page treasure trove of Beasties material including interviews, memoir, photos, recipes, and a comic strip.

TOP ALBUM *Ill Communication* (1994) For "Sabotage" alone this would be my favorite Beasties' record, but it also contains "Sure Shot" (which samples a talking dog), "Root Down," and some seriously funky instrumentals, including "Futterman's Rule" and "Sabrosa."

POP TRIVIA In the '90s, the Beastie Boys were multimedia moguls. They started their own record label, Grand Royal, and published a magazine of the same name devoted to hip-hop, skate, and nerd culture. Mike D was also involved in founding the clothing brand, X-Large. In 2000, I went to New York for the first time and bought a T-shirt from the X-Large shop, fan boy that I am.

PUBLIC ENEMY

Public Enemy brought politics to hip-hop, fiercely articulating the experience of Black Americans facing institutional racism and socio-economic disadvantage.

The group formed in early '80s Long Island, New York, coalescing around outspoken frontman Chuck D, "hype man" Flavor Flav, and DJ Terminator X. The band's innovative production crew were dubbed The Bomb Squad (Public Enemy love a provocative title). From the start, their sound was harsh, industrial, full of hooks, but bordering on dissonance, incorporating samples from punk and metal as well as funk and soul.

Chuck D's lyrics often deal with the continued existence of racism in American culture and mass media, and encourage the Black community to achieve self-empowerment through an understanding of their history. Flavor Flav acts as the comedic counterpoint to all this seriousness, goofing around like a Shakespearean fool whenever things get a bit preachy.

Public Enemy's name and image perfectly supported their radical outlook. They adopted the imagery of the Black Panthers and name-checked Malcolm X and The Nation of Islam. They played with the terminology and appearance of militant political groups and proto-states, appointing rapper Professor Griff as "Minister for Information." On stage the band were flanked by the S1W (Security of the First World), a crew dressed in black military fatigues, red berets, and holding (fake) uzis. This made quite an impression in 1986 when Public Enemy supported their Def Jam label-mates the Beastie Boys (who were then known as beer-swigging frat boys). Some of the public consternation this generated is captured on "Incident At 66.6 FM" on 1990's *Fear of a Black Planet,* which is built around samples from a radio phone-in.

Public Enemy's first three albums, *Yo! Bum Rush the Show* (1987), *It Takes a Nation of Millions to Hold Us Back* (1988), and *Fear of a Black Planet* (1990), are all rap classics.

In February 2020 Chuck D and Flavor Flav dramatically fell out over Flav's refusal to play a campaign rally for Democratic candidate Bernie Sanders. Amid much public name-calling on social media Flav was kicked out of the band. Or was he? On April 1 Chuck D announced that the spat had been a hoax to raise the group's profile. It wasn't entirely clear that this had been explained to Flav. The album that followed soon after was credited to Enemy Radio (all of Public Enemy apart fom Flav) but Flav did appear on the single "Food as a Machine Gun."

TOP ALBUM *Fear of a Black Planet* (1990) "Welcome to the Terrordome" is one of the band's densest tracks, propelled by a relentless barrage of samples. Somewhere in that sonic soup you can just about make out Kool & the Gang's "Jungle Boogie"! On "911 is a Joke" Flavor Flav takes a main vocal, rapping about the slow response of ambulance crews to emergency calls in Black neighborhoods. And "Fight the Power" is perhaps the quintessential Public Enemy track. Originally composed for Spike Lee's 1989 film *Do The Right Thing,* it fizzes with rage, lollops along on the back of James Brown samples, and takes lyrical pop shots at America's white heroes, Elvis and John Wayne.

POP TRIVIA Innovative DJ, Terminator X, left the group in 1994, apparently to raise ostriches.

Flavor Flav is famous for wearing a clock round his neck and has said that this symbolizes the precious nature of each moment. An acquaintance who used to take photos for UK music paper the *NME* told me that Flav was several hours late for a photoshoot. Presumably his clock ran out of batteries.

Public Enemy had a late hit in the UK in 2012 with "Harder Than You Think" (which was originally from their 2007 album, *How You Sell Soul to a Soulless People Who Sold Their Soul?*). It was picked up as the theme tune to the 2012 Paralympic Games coverage on UK TV. The track susequently went to Number Five in the British charts—P.E.'s highest ever position in the UK. The uplifting brass motif is sampled from Shirley Bassey's 1972 song "Jezahel."

...THE SPEAKING CLOCK PROVIDED BY FLAVOR FLAV...

...AT THE THIRD STROKE, THE TIME WILL BE...

...11:35 AM...

YEEEEAH BOOOYYY!

THE POGUES

The Pogues combined the energy, DIY ethos, and confrontational attitude of punk with traditional Irish music. In the process, they introduced a generation of post-punk, rowdy music fans to... gasp... folk music.

The Pogues' take on Irish music wasn't twee or even respectful. It was full-blooded, bloody-minded, and frequently political. Their gigs were legendarily chaotic and trouble followed wherever they went. The band was largely made up of second-generation Irish Londoners and their material described the experience of contemporary and historical Irish emigrants, something that also connected with audiences in the US.

The band was formed by Shane MacGowan, Spider Stacy, and Jem Finer in London in 1977 and was originally called Pogue Mahone, an English transliteration of the Irish for "kiss my arse." Debut album *Red Roses for Me* (1984) is rambunctious, infectious stuff. The opening song "Transmetropolitan" is a foul-mouthed, drunken roister across London and "Streams of Whiskey" imagines meeting (and inevitably getting drunk with) deceased Irish playwright Brendan Behan.

Their next album, *Rum, Sodomy & the Lash* (1985), was produced by Elvis Costello (see page 25) and, again, featured a mixture of original compositions, covers, and traditional songs. *If I Should Fall from Grace with God* (1988) was the band's critical and commercial peak, featuring a greater breadth of styles and more sophisticated arrangements than previous albums. It included Philip Chevron's haunting ballad of Irish emigration, "Thousands Are Sailing," and the

deranged party tune, "Fiesta." The record also, of course, featured "Fairytale of New York," a duet with Kirsty MacColl that has become a much-loved alternative Christmas carol.

MacGowan's drinking made him increasingly unreliable both live and in the studio. The band managed two more albums with him, *Peace & Love* (1989) and *Hell's Ditch* (1990), before giving him the boot. They performed with The Clash's Joe Strummer on vocals for a while, until Spider Stacy took over for their final albums, *Waiting for Herb* (1993) and *Pogue Mahone* (1995). In 2001 The Pogues reformed (with MacGowan) and have toured and performed sporadically since. Jem Finer moved into experimental music, while MacGowan has recorded and toured with his band The Popes—he is somehow still alive.

TOP ALBUM *Rum Sodomy & the Lash* (1985) Named after a description of the Royal Navy apocryphally attributed to Winston Churchill, this has the dangerous mania of early Pogues, but also some of their most melancholic moments, including the devastating rent-boy lament "The Old Main Drag." It also boasts a beautiful interpretation of "Dirty Old Town," written by Kirsty's dad, Ewan MacColl.

POP TRIVIA An on-going subplot to the musical career of The Pogues has been the decaying tragedy of MacGowan's teeth. After a lifetime of oral self-abuse, the last of Shane's stumps bit the dust in 2008. In 2015 the miraculous dental reconstruction of Shane MacGowan made an unlikely Christmas documentary on Sky Arts. We must now get used to the alarming sight of MacGowan with a full set of pearly white dentures.

DEPECHE MODE

Depeche Mode were one of the most influential electronic bands of the 1980s and '90s. Their sound developed from simple synth-pop to the complex, somber compositions of their later albums.

Depeche Mode formed in 1981 in Essex, modeling themselves on early influences: Ultravox and Orchestral Manoeuvres in the Dark. Vince Clarke wrote the majority of the songs on their debut album, *Speak and Spell* (1981), including upbeat electro-earworm, "Just Can't Get Enough." After Clarke left the band to form Yazoo (and later Erasure), the band's main songwriting duties were inherited by sensitive, blonde mop-top, Martin Gore.

After post-Clarke album *A Broken Frame* (1982), they recruited Alan Wilder, who brought a new musical versatility to Gore's compositions. On *Construction Time Again* (1983) the band developed a more industrial sound, incorporating samples of mechanical noises. The album was recorded at West Berlin's legendary Hansa Studios (where Bowie and Eno had recorded much of *Heroes* and *Low*). Gore's songwriting became more personal and daring in its subject matter. *Some Great Reward* (1984) featured gay anthem "People Are People" and "Master and Servant," a BDSM-flaunting vamp that features synthetic whip and chain sound effects. Early photos show fresh-faced lads in slacks who look like they've bunked off school to play *Top of the Pops*, but by now the band were in black leather. Gore, in particular, would perform kitted out in bondage straps and studs.

The band continued to develop their dark, moody synth sounds on albums *Black Celebration* (1986) and *Music for the Masses* (1987). *Violator* (1990) was their darkest record yet, featuring the hit "Personal Jesus" (see below), and was followed by Number One album *Songs of Faith and Devotion* (1993). Influenced by the contemporary sounds of grunge, the band was now mixing the electronics with guitars. Unfortunately, Dave Gahan took another lesson from grunge and became addicted to heroin. At the height of their powers, the band appeared to be falling apart.

Against the odds the band stayed together, although Wilder left in 1995—so returning them to the post-Clarke line-up of Gore, Gahan, and Andy Fletcher. The band has released five albums since 1997 and toured to enormous audiences all over the world.

TOP ALBUM *Violator* (1990) There are lots of synths, but this ain't synth-pop no more. Here the band weaves a dark spell of brooding, sexual menace. There are hooks aplenty, squelchy electronic bass, and backing vocals that hint at gospel. "Personal Jesus" is, of course, an absolute stonker, owing as much to glam rock as it does to grunge.

POP TRIVIA To publicize the release of "Personal Jesus," the marketing wonks at Mute Records hit upon an ingenious campaign. They placed ads in the personal sections of UK regional newspapers with the phrase: "Your own personal Jesus." Later versions of the ad included a phone number, which you could ring to hear the song.

R.E.M.

R.E.M. might just be the most influential American band of the 1980s. Like The Smiths in the UK, they became the archetypal independent band, encouraging not so much slavish imitation as an individual, artistic spirit in other bands.

Like Johnny Marr, R.E.M. co-founder Peter Buck was inspired by folk and rock artists of the '60s and '70s, such as The Byrds and Big Star, and his jangly, arpeggiated guitar playing is one of the band's signature qualities. The other is Michael Stipe's distinctive, high vibrato, which is somewhat reminiscent of Neil Young's voice (see page 27).

The band formed in Atlanta, Georgia, in 1980 and released their first single, "Radio Free Europe," on local label Hib-Tone in 1981. Their first album, *Murmur* (1983), was a cult hit, which established the early R.E.M. sound of jangly guitar rock with Stipe's enigmatic vocals. His oblique, poetic lyrics were particularly inspired by the lyrical approach of Patti Smith (see page 28). They recorded three albums over the next three years, including a stint in London with Nick Drake's producer, Joe Boyd. In 1987 they released their last album for I.R.S. Records, *Document* (see below), and signed with Warner Bros. on the condition of creative freedom.

Green (1988), their first record for Warner Bros., saw the band deliberately experimenting with a wide variety of styles. In retrospect, you can see intimations of the sounds they would perfect in their megastar years. Wry pop songs "Stand" and "Pop Song 89" look forward to "Shiny Happy People" and "Man on the Moon"; "You Are the Everything" and "Hairshirt" anticipate the folk arrangements of "Losing My Religion" and "Find the River"; and halfway through "World Leader Pretend" you can practically hear the piano part from "Nightswimming."

Over the course of their next two albums they made good on these experiments. *Out of Time* (1991) propelled the band to international stardom, with "Losing my Religion" and "Shiny Happy People" inescapable on radio and MTV. *Automatic for the People* (1992) pushed things even further, making them the biggest band in the world for a while. Its most famous song, "Everybody Hurts," written mainly by drummer Bill Berry, became an anthem of triumph over emotional pain.

There was no way that R.E.M. could maintain that level of success, nor I would imagine did they want to. They responded to *Automatic for the People*'s folk and orchestral arrangements by making an all-out rock record, *Monster* (1994), filled with glam-rock fuzz guitar. Thereafter, they continued as they always had, making albums that followed their own inclination, veering between pop and artier, experimental phases. In 1997 Bill Berry left the band and they continued as a three-piece (Stipe, Buck, and bassist Mike Mills). The following album, *Up* (1998), sold relatively poorly, but contains my favorite R.E.M. song, the gorgeous "Daysleeper." They released their 15th and final album, *Collapse into Now*, in 2011 and announced the end of the band later that year. Peter Buck has released solo records and albums with other bands since R.E.M., including 2020's *Beat Poetry for the Survivalist* with British maverick Luke Haines.

TOP ALBUM *Document* (1987) This was R.E.M.'s last album for I.R.S. and perhaps, as a result, was their most uncompromising record yet. It sounded rockier than previous releases and was lyrically more direct, particularly on overtly political songs "Welcome to the Occupation" and "Exhuming McCarthy," which criticized the Reagan administration. But it was also their mainstream breakthrough, producing hit single "The One I Love" and "It's the End of the World As We Know It (and I Feel Fine)."

POP TRIVIA Stipe's lyrics make numerous references to other musicians, artists, and performers, including Lenny Bruce and Andy Kaufman. "What's the Frequency, Kenneth?", from *Monster* (1994), takes its title from a recurring line in Daniel Clowes' terrifying graphic novel *Like a Velvet Glove Cast in Iron*, originally published in his comic *Eightball*.

CHAPTER THREE

THE Nineties STAGE

FEATURING THE FOLLOWING ARTISTS:

WU-TANG CLAN
björk
blur
Sterolab
PULP
DJ SHADOW
massive attack
NIRVANA
oasis
PJ Harvey
JEFF BUCKLEY

PAVEMENT
THE STONE ROSES
Primal Scream
RADIOHEAD
NICK CAVE AND THE BAD SEEDS
the chemical brothers
APHEX TWIN
daft punk
BECK
Belle and Sebastian
SUPER FURRY ANIMALS

DANCE ★ TRIP HOP ★ GRUNGE ★ ROCK ★ BRIT POP

WU-TANG CLAN

It would probably take more space than I have here to list all the members and affiliates of the Wu-Tang Clan, let alone give any kind of potted history of their sprawling network of projects, prolific releases, and bizarre behavior. Suffice it to say that their music (particularly the production-style of de facto leader RZA) and their image and attitude were enormously influential on hip-hop in the 1990s and beyond.

The Wu-Tang Clan formed in the early '90s in Staten Island, New York. The original members were (here goes) RZA, GZA, Method Man, Raekwon, Ghostface Killah, Inspectah Deck, U-God, Masta Killa, and Ol' Dirty Bastard. Named after the martial arts film *Shaolin and Wu Tang,* their love of martial arts imagery was all over 1993 debut album *Enter the Wu-Tang (36 Chambers),* both in its lyrics and samples. RZA oversaw the production of the album. After its release he initiated the next phase of his "five year plan," producing solo records for each member of the Clan. I don't even know where to start with this lot. Totting up the collaborative and solo efforts over 20 years takes you to well over 60 studio albums. The Wu's business model proved to be as influential as their music. The collective structure enabled them to form a sprawling Wu-Tang media empire with artists making solo albums or collaborating in various configurations and periodically reuniting to make the big group record.

This also had the effect of creating an ongoing soap opera in which various members had spats with artists from within or outside the Clan. Ol' Dirty Bastard's erratic behavior was the source of many strange stories. He was in prison during the making of the group's third album, *The W* (2000), but managed literally to phone in a performance all the same. He later went on the run from the police, narrowly evading capture when he appeared at the launch party for *The W.* Later albums mixed the Shaolin stylings with political and religious views derived from the Five Percent Nation, an offshoot of the Nation of Islam. In 1999, RZA composed the soundtrack for Jim Jarmusch's *Ghost Dog: The Way of the Samurai,* a movie that it is fair to say was probably right up his street.

TOP ALBUM *Enter the Wu-Tang (36 Chambers)* (1993) is an abrasive collision of martial arts quotes, foul-mouthed raps, woozy jazz, soul samples, and heavy bass. Its production style was a big influence on subsequent East Coast hip-hop artists, including Nas and Jay-Z.

POP TRIVIA In 2015 Wu-Tang released one copy only of their new album *Once Upon a Time in Shaolin....* It was auctioned with legal conditions that prevented it being commercially exploited until 2103. It was later revealed that the successful bidder was pharmaceutical CEO Martin Shkreli (dubbed at the time "the most hated man in America" for raising the price of the drug Daraprim by over 5,000 percent), who bought the one-off album for $2 million. The Wu were not best pleased on finding out the identity of their mystery buyer, entering into a public war of words with Shkreli, who Ghostface Killah labeled "the man with the 12-year-old body."

Wu-Tang released their eighth studio album *The Saga Continues* in 2017, produced by group DJ Mathematics. In 2019, Hulu broadcast Wu-Tang: *An American Saga*, a fictionalised account of the group's origin.

björk

Check out Kristen Wiig's hilarious impressions on *Saturday Night Live* to see how people still think of Björk— the strange pixie girl from Iceland, that fairy-tale nation whose main exports are "fishing, dragons, and screaming."

If you dig a little deeper you will discover that Björk is everything a modern musician should be. She fearlessly explores new musical territory, taking bits of rock, pop, folk, classical, choral, techno, hip-hop, trip-hop, house, and performance art and incorporating them into her inventive compositions. Think Bowie in the 1970s or Kate Bush in the '80s for a comparison to her adventurous musical spirit.

Björk came to prominence in the late '80s as part of eccentric Icelandic band The Sugarcubes, but her real breakthrough was the 1993 solo album *Debut*. She had moved to London with her young son and (presumably with the help of a good babysitter) embraced the UK dance scene. Björk recruited Massive Attack producer Nellee Hooper to help her craft the big beats and eclectic sounds of *Debut*. But it was her voice that made the biggest impression—her strange inflections, caught somewhere between Reykjavík and East London, the girlish voice that would hiccup and burble, then swell into a powerful roar.

Her follow-up album, *Post* (1995), was a similarly diverse and dancey affair, and Björk became an unlikely '90s pop star, reaching an MTV audience through clever videos directed by Michel Gondry and Spike Jonze. After a brush with a disturbed fan, she retreated a little from public scrutiny and the British tabloid press. *Homogenic* (1997) was a more organic, focused album and a deliberate attempt to reflect her homeland and to create a modern Icelandic pop music (see right).

Björk has continued to make innovative albums, though her music has moved further away from chart-pleasing hits. Lyrically she's moved between the conceptual and the intensely personal, working with a bewildering variety of collaborators that includes Mark Bell, Mike Patton, Antony Hegarty, Robert Wyatt, Matmos, Toumani Diabaté, Alexander McQueen, and British TV's national treasure Sir David Attenborough. *Biophilia* (2011) was a huge multimedia project released as an album and a series of interactive apps. It developed out of Björk's fascination with science and the natural world, and explored aspects of biology, geology, virology, and cosmology. The live performances of *Biophilia* incorporated new musical instruments invented for the occasion, including the "gameleste" and the brilliantly named "gravity harp." *Vulnicura* (2015) is as personal as its predecessor was conceptual. It was Björk's typically original version of a break-up album, dwelling on her split from Matthew Barney, film artist and

the father of her daughter. Her next album reacted against its moody predecessor—*Utopia* (2017) is true to its name, blooming with lush orchestration, bird calls and trilling flutes. The videos and album artwork feature some of Björk's weirdest imagery yet—I'm calling this look "Vaginal Bird Embryo Flute Goblin." In 2018 and 2019 she toured Europe and America with her lavish Cornucopia production.

TOP ALBUMS *Debut* (1993) This isn't technically Björk's debut, as she recorded a solo album at the age of 12. Still, it's the moment she launched herself as a solo artist, with modern pop gems such as "Human Behaviour," "Venus As A Boy," and "Big Time Sensuality."

Homogenic (1997) This album rolls over Iceland's volcanic landscape in epic sweeps, somehow meshing a folky, natural feel with modern, computerized beats. Björk recruited Icelandic poet Sjón to help capture this epic feeling in the lyrics for "Jóga" and "Bachelorette." The album was also her first collaboration with producer and electronic musician Mark Bell, a musical relationship that continued until his tragically early death in 2014.

POP TRIVIA Björk's incredible outfits are as celebrated as her music. She has worked with cutting-edge fashion designers to create a look appropriate to each album. The late Alexander McQueen designed the fierce "warrior-geisha" look for the cover of *Homogenic*. At the 2001 Academy Awards, she famously wore a dress resembling a wraparound swan and "laid" eggs on the red carpet.

She composed the music for, and reluctantly starred in, Lars von Trier's misery-musical *Dancer in the Dark* (2000). The atmosphere on set became so fraught that Björk reportedly ate one of her costumes. Still, that's according to the famously mischievous Von Trier, so should perhaps be taken with a pinch of salt.

blur

In which, dear reader, we must address the union-flagged elephant in the room, the beer-swilling specter of... *Britpop*.

It's all too easy to cringe now, but it started out as a genuinely interesting exploration of the foibles of what singer Damon Albarn would later describe as "this stroppy little island of mixed-up people." And it wasn't just Blur. The Britpop monicker was an attempt by the UK music press to shoehorn several bands, notably Suede and The Auteurs, into a recognizable scene. All of these bands were, to say the least, ambivalent about "Britishness" and the nation's cultural history. Blur drew on the 1960s observational vignettes of The Kinks and the barbed dispatches of XTC (see page 65) to write songs full of lost, lonely, stressed Londoners. Which isn't to say that there wasn't also something celebratory going on. Blur's musical style in the early '90s was in no small part a reaction to the popularity of grunge and Nirvana (see page 84), a slightly pissy feeling that us Brits should stop listening to the Yanks and remember all the great British bands who had gone before. But pop music is weirdly good at ambivalence, and Blur wrote songs that were simultaneously celebratory and critical, exuberant and yet depressed. Once you're made the figurehead of a "movement," these subtleties get a bit lost, but to criticize Blur as being loutish apologists for "Cool Britannia" is to make the same mistake as every US presidential wannabe who's wanted to use "Born in the USA" as his campaign song.

Blur were always cleverer and more interesting than that. Debut album *Leisure* (1991) is an unfocused record of the band playing with their influences, oscillating between Syd Barrett, My Bloody Valentine, and the then-in-vogue "baggy" sound. It does, however, include pop gem "There's No Other Way" and the beautiful lament "Birthday." *Modern Life Is Rubbish* (1993) is the album where it all came together. Born out of financial crisis, with the band on the verge of splitting up, they found their sound and Albarn found his lyrical voice, describing modern, urban alienation. *Parklife* (1994) was THE BIG ONE, which propelled them to stardom in the UK. If you grew up in the '90s, it's hard to divorce *Parklife* from the era it came to represent, but it *is* a great album, an eclectic set of poised songs, from club banger ("Girls & Boys") to '60s pop ("End Of A Century") and French chanson ("To The End"). *The Great Escape* (1995) is a weird record—on the one hand it's experimental and pushes beyond a national focus, on the other it's very "laddish." This split personality is represented by its title, which is both a jingoistic allusion to plucky Second World War Brits and a paranoid plea to escape the pressures of fame.

From there on, Blur did just that, retreating from the boorish Britpop monster they had helped create and re-engaging (at least more overtly) with their artier tendencies. For a band that had once publicly defined themselves in opposition to US alt-rock, they now embraced all things lo-fi and fuzzy (Pixies, Pavement, and guitarist Graham Coxon's beloved Dinosaur Jr.) and 1997's *Blur* brought them their biggest international hit, "Song 2" and the haunting "Beetlebum." They pushed further down this noisy, experimental furrow on 1999's *13* and recorded *Think Tank* (2003) without Coxon, before going on indefinite hiatus.

In the meantime, Albarn invented the hugely successful Gorillaz. Cards on the table, Blur are my favorite band and Jamie Hewlett (co-creator of *Tank Girl*) is one of my favorite comic artists. So when I discovered that Hewlett and Albarn were collaborating, it seemed as if they were making something just for me! Gorillaz were the ultimate manufactured band, pushing the idea of a cartoon music group, à la The Archies, as

far as time and animation budgets would allow.. Once criticized for musical parochialism, Gorillaz showed Albarn riffing off everything from hip-hop, dub, and ska to Cuban, African, and Arab music, and collaborating with a who's who of musicians, including De La Soul (see page 62), Gruff Rhys (see page 105), and Lou Reed (see page 16)) and an ever growing roll call of young, cutting edge, rappers and singers.

Of course, Blur had a happy ending. Gradually levered apart by the pressures of fame, musical disagreements, and personal problems, the band fizzled out after *Think Tank*. Thankfully, Albarn and Coxon rekindled their friendship and the band reunited to play gigs in 2009. After single releases in 2010 and 2012, they released a new album, *The Magic Whip*, in 2015. Based on recordings while on tour in Hong Kong in 2013, the album was largely pieced together by Coxon and their main producer in the '90s, Stephen Street. It. Is. Really. Good.

TOP ALBUM *Modern Life Is Rubbish* (1993) is probably still my favorite album ever. It's the sound of a band finding their feet, their sound, and their subject. On "Advert," "Colin Zeal," "Star Shaped," and "Chemical World," you can hear them alchemically transforming all the frustration, disappointment, and alcoholic exhaustion into great pop music. "For Tomorrow" contains some of Albarn's most lovely lyrics, and Coxon's guitar-playing throughout hits a transcendent sweet spot between punky abrasion and melody.

POP TRIVIA The members of Blur have kept themselves busy. Graham Coxon has released eight excellent solo albums (including my favorite *The Spinning Top* in 2009) and composed music for Netflix drama *The End of the F***ing World*. Apart from Gorillaz, Damon Albarn has formed at least two other bands, written music for three dramatic productions, and started Africa Express, a project to facilitate collaboration between African and Western musicians. A joke in British comic *Viz* ran that Albarn had gone to the toilet and by the time he emerged had started two new bands with the toilet bleach and the hand-dryer. Drummer Dave Rowntree retrained as a solicitor and stood for UK Parliament as a Labour candidate. Bassist Alex James moved to a very big house in the country and became a cheesemaker.

DAMON ALBARN IS NOW SO PROLIFIC...

...HIS MUSICAL ACTIVITY IS VISIBLE FROM SPACE.

HOUSTON, IT LOOKS LIKE IT'S...

IS THERE ANYONE OUT THERE?

...FORMING A MESSAGE!

WANNA MAKE AN ALBUM?

Stereolab

Stereolab were a pioneering, genre-melting Anglo-French band that formed in 1990. They wore their influences on their sleeve, but mixed them up to create something uniquely their own. One of the first bands to be described as "post-rock," this term fails to do justice to how fun they were.

In the '90s, against the backdrop of grunge and Britpop, Stereolab sounded impossibly exotic, like European space jazz from the future. Stereolab's founders were Laetitia Sadier and Tim Gane who were a couple, as well as a songwriting partnership, for most of the band's career. They sounded nothing like other bands of the era. Instead of verse/chorus/verse and guitar solos, they built throbbing audio loops around Krautrock motorik drum patterns and were retro-tech geeks before anyone else remembered what a Moog was. Sadier, in particular, was a fantasy figure of European sophistication for a generation of provincial indie kids (or maybe that was just me). She coolly intoned her vocals in the manner of a modern-day chanteuse, but, if you tuned into her hypnotic lyrics, you might get a brief lecture in leftist cyclical economic theory, as in 1994's "Ping Pong." Again it's that trick of wrapping a serious subject in catchy pop clothing but, as with many other practitioners of this technique (Morrissey, Pulp, Elvis Costello), there was also a mischievous sense of humor at play here.

Early Stereolab songs tended toward a Krautrock sound, with keyboard drones and rhythmic guitars, as on 1992's *Peng*. 1993's *The Groop Played Space Age Batchelor Pad Music* (Stereolab always gave good titles) added easy listening influences to the mix. Later that year they released *Transient Random Noise Bursts With Announcements* (as I said, good titles) and the fan-favorite song (as a B-side!) "French Disko," which combined the mechanical and melodic sides of their sound to great effect. As the band developed, their sound became less abrasive and more melodically sophisticated.

Perhaps their two most accessible albums, *Mars Audiac Quintet* (1994) and *Emperor Tomato Ketchup* (1996), show the increasing influence of lounge music, jazz, Europop, and Burt Bacharach, combining complex time signatures with apparent melodic simplicity.

The longest-standing member of the band, apart from Sadier and Gane, was Mary Hansen, who played guitar and keyboards as well as singing backing vocals. Her harmonies and ability to weave in and out of Sadier's vocals created distinctive vocal arrangements,. In 2002, she was tragically killed in a traffic accident. Stereolab continued until 2009, before taking an indefinite break. They released a final album, *Not Music*, in 2010. Sadier has released three solo albums since 2010 and Gane has formed the band Cavern of Anti-Matter. In 2019 Stereolab reformed to tour Europe and the US.

TOP ALBUM *Sound-Dust* (2001) This album has both sides of Stereolab—the experimental and pop tendencies—in spades. There are weird time signatures that phase in and out, moog oscillations, warm brass arrangements, jazz flute, and Star Trek vocals. Second song on the album, "Spacemoth," is a mini-symphony in itself, segueing from Twilight Zone suspense into spooky French chanson into upbeat cocktail soul. Then, a pause, a drum fill, and it kicks into "Captain Easychord," the funkiest thing they ever wrote.

POP TRIVIA Laetitia Sadier provided backing vocals in French for Blur's chanson-inspired "To The End" on their 1994 album *Parklife* (see page 78).

PULP

While today Jarvis Cocker resembles a musical Stephen Fry—an amiable guide to the arts on BBC Radio—as singer and lyricist for Pulp he was like Philip Larkin crossed with Serge Gainsbourg, a gimlet-eyed geek with the permanent horn.

Cocker had spent years in the indie wilderness, shouting about sex and polyester to no avail. The stars finally aligned in 1992 when Pulp's wry take on urban, kitchen-sink sexual mores struck a chord with a newly Brit-obsessed music press and public. From 1992 they released a terrific string of singles that started with "O.U." and included "Babies", a sex drama in miniature, and "Razzmatazz", a comic-tragic put-down of an ex, as sad as it is cruel. "Sheffield Sex City" is Cocker on heat, stalking his hometown to a housey bassline.

This, ahem, purple period culminated in their breakthrough album, *His 'n' Hers* in 1994. Their popularity peaked with the release of "Common People," in 1995. It was an instant anthem, its sarcastic criticism of class tourism particularly apposite in an era when middle-class kids developed cockney and Mancunian accents over night. That year they triumphantly headlined at Glastonbury and released their hit album *Different Class*, which included "Common People" and "Disco 2000." *This Is Hardcore* (1998) was a darker album than its predecessor, dealing with the fall-out of fame. Cocker's lustful urges reached their grubby, compulsive conclusion in the weary (and brilliant) title track.

Pulp recorded one more album, 2001's intermittently great *We Love Life*, produced by alternative music legend Scott Walker, before calling it a day. In 2012 the band reformed to tour, and in 2013 they released a single "After You," produced by LCD Soundsystem's James Murphy (see page 122). Jarvis has released two solo albums and a collaborative album with Chilly Gonzales. His current band, the punningly named JARV IS, released their first album *Beyond the Pale* in 2020.

TOP ALBUM *His 'n' Hers* (1994) *Different Class* (1995) is the one with the hits, but for me *His 'n' Hers* is Pulp at the peak of their powers. The music is a fizzy, synthetic mix of funk, disco, and pop hooks that sounds thrillingly unlike meat-and-two-veg guitar bands in 1994.

POP TRIVIA In the '90s Cocker stood out due to his distinct personal style. I went to see Pulp in the early '90s with my friend Steve. We knew we liked the music but we didn't know much about the band. Watching the support band in front of us was a tall skinny guy in vintage clothing. "Where'd he get his clothes? Oxfam?" we mocked. When Pulp took to the stage we realized that the skinny guy was, of course, Jarvis, and we felt like the judgmental idiots we were. Now I would give my hind teeth for a loan from Jarvis' wardrobe.

DJ SHADOW

DJ Shadow is known for atmospheric, instrumental hip-hop, woven together from diverse samples of music, obscure TV shows, documentaries, and adverts. He makes hip-hop for the head and it was equally cerebral musicians Radiohead (see page 94) who helped to popularize him in the UK.

The wordless nature of much of DJ Shadow's music (apart from sampled spoken passages and snatches of song) means his tracks aren't limited to typical song structures or lengths. They develop over longer time periods, growing into moody soundscapes that at times bring him close to contemporary classical music.

DJ Shadow (real name Josh Davis) began DJ'ing at the University of California. In the early '90s, he collaborated with Blackalicious and MCs such as Lyrics Born under the banner of the Solesides collective (which later grew into the larger collective and record label Quannum Projects). His first album was *Endtroducing...* (1996), a stunning record that seemed to arrive as a fully formed proposal for a new kind of music (see below). This is still the record for which he is most renowned.

Fans had to wait until 2002 for his second album *The Private Press*. It was another atmospheric soup of samples, song fragments, and repurposed clips, but failed to reach the heights of *Endtroducing...*, either in its execution or critical reception. On 2006's *The Outsider* he chose to wrong-foot people's expectations by producing an album of actual rap tracks. It delved into the San Francisco Bay "hyphy" scene, featuring local rappers as well as A Tribe Called Quest veteran Q-Tip and fellow Quannum alumnus Lateef the Truthspeaker. 2011's *The Less You Know, The Better* featured guest appearances from Talib Kweli, Tom Vek, and Little Dragon and mixed instrumentals with more conventional song structures, often featuring sampled vocals. DJ Shadow has continued this collaborative approach on two subsequent albums, *The Mountain Will Fall* (2016) and *Our Pathetic Age* (2019), featuring performances from De La Soul (see page 62), Run the Jewels, Ghostface Killah, Raekwon (see page 75) and Nas.

He has also collaborated on other projects beyond his own records. In the '90s he forged a relationship with James Lavelle, founder of Mo' Wax records, and produced Unkle's debut *Psyence Fiction* (1998), a trip-hop album with guest vocals from the great and the good of UK and US alternative music, including Thom Yorke (see page 94) and Mike D (see page 66).

TOP ALBUM *Endtroducing...* (1996) Twenty years on, this album still sounds like nothing else. Using only a sampler, a turntable, and a tape recorder, he painstakingly built its melancholy, atmospheric tracks from the flotsam of late-20th-century pop culture. The album isn't built entirely from samples, as there are small vocal contributions from friends Gift of Gab and Lyrics Born. Nevertheless, it's an incredible achievement. He samples everything from Björk to *Twin Peaks*, repurposing them into new sonic structures. Listening to the album as a whole is essential, but my personal highlights are "Organ Donor" (built around a Giorgio Moroder sample and sounds like Bach having a breakdown in a church) and "Midnight in a Perfect World," which lifts its sad piano motif from David Axelrod's jazz tribute to William Blake, "The Human Abstract."

POP TRIVIA DJ Shadow apparently has over 60,000 records—and presumably a very good filing system.

massive attack

Along with other Bristolians Portishead and Tricky, Massive Attack pioneered what became known as trip-hop, a laid-back, dub- and dope-influenced take on hip-hop originating in the west of England.

Massive Attack was started by Mushroom (Andy Vowles), Daddy G (Grant Marshall), and 3D (Robert Del Naja). Their first album, *Blue Lines* (1991), sounded thrillingly different—jazzy, but disjointed, with drugged-out raps in Bristolian accents over dubby basslines. The album's hit single "Unfinished Sympathy" added pop sparkle, its epic sweeping strings and Shara Nelson's vocal making it as much a modern take on soul as hip-hop. Early on they established the pattern of inviting guest vocalists to record with them, combining song with raps from 3D, Daddy G, and other local luminaries, in particular Tricky. Repeating this formula on *Protection* (1994), they recruited Tracey Thorn to sing the lead track and also worked with Björk's producer Nellee Hooper. On 1998's *Mezzanine* the Cocteau Twins' Elizabeth Fraser guested on "Teardrop," a song that sounds both beautiful and fearful, as if Fraser is singing to keep someone alive over the backing beat of a life-support machine. Massive Attack's sound, driven particularly by 3D, was becoming increasingly chilly and insomniac-like, and incorporated stylistic influences from rock and punk. Communication within the group had become fractured, with all three members working independently in the studio, and Mushroom left the group in 1999.

2003's *100th Window* was a collaboration between 3D and producer Neil Davidge, featuring vocals from Horace Andy and Sinead O'Connor. In a nod to Massive Attack's influence on his post-Blur work, Damon Albarn's backing vocals are credited to Gorillaz' 2D. Albarn also collaborated with 3D and Daddy G for songs on fifth album *Heligoland* (2010), along with Tunde Adebimpe from TV On the Radio (see page 111), and Guy Garvey from Elbow (see page 127). In 2016 Massive Attack released two EP's. *Ritual Spirit* featured Roots Manuva, Young Fathers, and their first collaboration with Tricky since 1994's *Protection*, while *The Spoils* boasted performances from Mazzy Star's Hope Sandoval and UK rapper Ghostpoet.

TOP ALBUM *Protection* (1994) This album takes the sound of their debut but pushes it further. "Euro Child" and "Spying Glass" are blissfully dubbed out, while the title track hints at the iciness that would dominate later records. "Karmacoma" sounds like it's 3am and 3D and Tricky have smoked a massive bag of weed. Its percussive soundscape points to the full-blown paranoid ramblings of Tricky's debut, *Maxinquaye*, released the next year.

POP TRIVIA Massive Attack's distinctive visual identity is largely down to 3D, who is also a graffiti artist. His paintings, which draw on street art as well as painters such as Francis Bacon, have adorned Massive Attack releases, as well as War Child's 1995 charity album *Help*.

NIRVANA

What can you say about Nirvana that hasn't already been said? They were a visceral force of nature, combining angry, distorted rock with melody in a sound that is only obvious in retrospect.

Kurt Cobain became a figurehead for angsty problem kids everywhere and then (probably) blew his brains out, joining the "dead stupidly young" gang of rock stars. Were they really the greatest band ever? Well, they were pretty bloody good and imagine what they might have gone *on* to do.

Cobain and bassist Krist Novoselic formed Nirvana in Seattle in the late 80s, influenced by US punk bands, including local heroes The Melvins and Mudhoney. They recorded their first album *Bleach* for local grunge label Sub Pop in 1989 with drummer Chad Channing. Cobain later expressed dissatisfaction with the sound of this album, complaining that Sub Pop had forced them to adopt a more consciously "rock" sound. Ironically, this forced the band to find their early signature sound, mixing punk rock with the classic-rock-riffage of Black Sabbath (see page 14) and Aerosmith. Cobain's more poppy predilections are also evident, though, particularly on the jangly "About A Girl."

In 1990, Dave Grohl took over as drummer, adding new muscle to their sound. They were bought out of their Sub Pop contract by major label DGC Records and recorded a promising little album with Butch Vig. ~~Nevermind sold disappointingly, hobbled by a poorly received single, "Smells Like Teen Spirit"...~~ "Smells Like Teen Spirit" was a surprise hit and *Nevermind* (1991) became an all-conquering behemoth, knocking Michael Jackson of the US Number One spot. Nirvana, and particularly Cobain, became very famous very quickly. *Nevermind* is one of those albums that is impossible to divorce from its era, but it still holds up. In addition to "Teen Spirit," "In Bloom," "Lithium," and "On A Plain" have become modern rock classics. The album pushed grunge rock into newly melodic territory and absorbed the Pixies' (see page 58) knack for effective dynamic contrasts. It also showcases the growing eclecticism of the band's tastes. Acoustic number "Polly" sits cheek by jowl with frantic thrasher "Territorial Pissings."

It's something of an understatement to say that Cobain struggled with his newly found fame. The band elected to record *Nevermind*'s eagerly anticipated follow-up with self-proclaimed "recording engineer" (don't call him a producer) Steve Albini, who had produced—dammit, I mean recorded—the Pixies's *Surfer Rosa* (1988). *In Utero* (1993) is full of cynical and self-mocking references to teenage angst and selling out, and is a deliberately uncompromising record, both in its sound and imagery ("Rape Me," anyone?). That same year the band recorded a largely acoustic performance for *MTV Unplugged*, later released as *MTV Unplugged in New York* (1994). They chose to perform their less well-known songs, as well as covers, introducing Generation X kids to Leadbelly's "Where Did You Sleep Last Night?" and David Bowie's "The Man Who Sold The World."

In early 1994 the band's European tour was cut short because of Cobain's drug and health problems. He checked into rehab to get off heroin but failed to complete the treatment. On April 8, he was found dead at his home in Seattle. What killed him? Not Courtney Love, not the Illuminati, just drugs, mental illness, and the stupid pressures of fame.

Nirvana was easily the best of the grunge bands. They revitalized rock music in a manner similar to punk, stripping back the bollocks to reveal angry, direct, powerful bursts of self-expression. Kurt Cobain has become a tragic messiah of self-destructive rock 'n' roll, which is almost certainly entirely missing the point. Along with R.E.M. (see page 72), Nirvana opened new ears to the left-field and off-kilter, but simultaneously changed the whole notion of "alternative music." If a band so resolutely opposed to the mainstream could become megastars, what was "alternative music" meant to be alternative *to*? From then on every tortured underground musician half-expected to become famous and every record label half-expected him to fulfil this unlikely promise. For better and for worse, they changed the nature of the game. *Nevermind* (1991) has sold over 30 million copies worldwide and Nirvana's name and logo continue to sell t-shirts and baby-grows.

TOP ALBUM *In Utero* (1993) Nirvana reacted against the success of *Nevermind* (1991) by recording this angrier, scarier album. Everything about it is a deliberately perverse reaction against the earlier record, from the disturbing artwork (the cynical song titles ("Radio Friendly Unit Shifter") and the self-mocking echo of "Smells Like Teen Spirit" at the beginning of "Rape Me." But the biggest impact comes from the bruising sound of the band at full throttle. They had grown tired of the polished production of *Nevermind* and hired Steve Albini to give *In Utero* a raw, live sound, with fewer overdubs. Which is not to say that it's *all* punishing guitars and screaming (though "Scentless Apprentice" and "Very Ape" definitely fit that bill). "Dumb" is a tender, sad little thing and "All Apologies" and "Heart-Shaped Box" are, for all their self-loathing and bile, catchy pop songs.

POP TRIVIA After Nirvana, Dave Grohl stepped out from behind the drum kit and formed a *second* world-straddling rock band, the Foo Fighters. For someone who was in such a legendarily angsty band, he also seems to have pulled off the trick of being the happiest and *nicest* man in rock. In addition to fronting Foo Fighters, he has played drums for acts that include Josh Homme's Queens of the Stone Age (see page 110), supergroup Them Crooked Vultures (with Homme and John Paul Jones), Tenacious D, and... The Muppets. How does he keep his energy up? Do yourself a favor and google "Dave Grohl, Fresh Pots." The man loves his coffee.

oasis

Brothers in bands, eh? That looks like hard work. Luckily, my brother's into classical, so it wasn't a problem for me. Though Noel and Liam Gallagher worshipped The Beatles to the point of tedium, the '60s icons they better resembled were The Kinks' Ray and Dave Davies, alternately driving each other on to great things or round the bend.

Oasis produced a lot of dross once they became famous, so it's illuminating to look at the early material and remember what a thrilling shot in the arm they were at the time. They slouched into the music press of the early '90s with serious attitude and it made perfect sense when they signed to the home of the big, bad rock 'n' rollers, Creation Records. Their arrogant-to-the-point-of-lunacy shtick was inherited from their more recent inspiration The Stone Roses (see page 92). In a way, they filled the hole that the Roses had left—of a mouthy, cool, Mancunian band—but Oasis were a harder-edged, more aggressive outfit.

Later on, during the (yawn) "Britpop wars," I chose Blur rather than Oasis, but I remember walking around school singing the latter's cool-as-f*** first single "Supersonic" to myself. It still sounds great, even if the nonsense lyrics now sound less like a surrealist pose and more like someone who can't be bothered. Their third single "Live Forever" established the other dominant sound of Oasis, the anthemic sing-along of vague euphoria, which the band would use to great effect on hordes of swaying, crying lads in football shirts in the years to come. Their debut album *Definitely Maybe* (1994)—the album titles got even worse later on—was an instant hit in the UK, being the fastest-selling debut in UK chart history at the time. It's probably still their best album, although I have a personal fondness for the follow-up (see right). It announces its intent from the very start with the cocksure "Rock 'n' Roll Star" and carries off its odes to hedonism ("Columbia" and "Cigarettes and Alcohol") with frazzled aplomb. Even their, ahem, borrowings from classic songs ("Shakermaker" lifted the melody from "I'd Like to Teach the World to Sing" and "Cigarettes and Alcohol" riffs on T. Rex's "Get It On") were part of the message, which was roughly: "We're not pissing about with all these bed-wetting indie bands, we're gonna be f***ing huge."

In 1995 the purported "Battle of Britpop" pitched Oasis' single "Roll With It" against Blur's "Country House." This undoubtedly helped both bands sell records but, in retrospect, polarized British alternative music into two artificial extremes—Oasis: northern, working class, emotional, and a bit thick; and Blur: southern, middle class, and too clever for

their own good. Though Blur won that puffed-up show of strength, Oasis' second album *(What's The Story) Morning Glory?* (1995) proved immensely popular and they went on to be the band with much broader appeal. In August 1996 they played two concerts at Knebworth, in Hertfordshire, performing to 125,000 people each day.

Unfortunately, the quality of their music developed an inverse relation to their popularity. *Be Here Now* (1997) was a gassy fart of an album, with overly long songs where nothing happened and titles that were inane even by Oasis' standards ("D'You Know What I Mean?," "It's Getting Better [Man!!]"). It must have sounded great if you'd had all the drugs. In 1999, Paul "Bonehead" Arthur and Paul McGuigan left the band, leaving the Gallaghers as the only original members. Gem Archer and Ride's Andy Bell came on board to play guitar and bass respectively. They released four more albums, but it's mainly crap from here on in, with an occasional pearl in all the manure. *Standing On The Shoulder Of Giants* (2000), named after a misremembered Isaac Newton quote that Noel Gallagher saw in the pub, sounds like Oasis trying to sound like anyone but themselves, chiefly The Stone Roses and The Beta Band. But it does have some decent moments of the band rocking out. Despite having the worst title of them all, *Don't Believe The Truth* (2005) is the best of their later albums, containing some properly exciting guitar playing and some good tunes untroubled by late-period overthinking. In 2009, while on tour, the Gallagher brothers finally, definitively, fell out and the group was no more. Liam Gallagher recorded two albums with Beady Eye (including Oasis alumni Gem Archer and Andy Bell) and has since released two solo albums. Noel Gallagher has released three solo albums with Noel Gallagher's High Flying Birds. Oasis will probably reform one day, beat the crap out of each other, and then split up again.

TOP ALBUM *(What's The Story) Morning Glory?* (1995) *Definitely Maybe* is probably a better album, but *Morning Glory* (as far as I know it has nothing to do with erections) is my favorite. I like Oasis when they stop trying to be The Beatles and play balls-out, loud rock music, and this album contains their most successful rock moment in the (almost) title track "Morning Glory." Album-closer "Champagne Supernova" is a genuinely epic piece of work, with a great guitar solo by Paul Weller (just try to ignore that stupid line about the cannon ball). And, yes, it may have been played to death and beyond, but "Wonderwall" is a lovely little thing.

POP TRIVIA Liam Gallagher has become an unlikely businessman after launching his own clothing range Pretty Green (named after a song by The Jam). The company now has a small chain of shops in the UK selling mod-inspired clothing, particularly suits and parkas. Liam is presumably not doing the sewing himself.

PJ Harvey

PJ Harvey has justly earned a reputation as an intense and exploratory songwriter, single-mindedly pursuing her lyrical and musical themes. Though her style has changed from album to album, a seam of darkness runs through her work.

PJ Harvey grew up in Dorset, in England's West Country, immersed in her parents' record collection of blues, Bob Dylan, and Captain Beefheart. These influences, along with later musical loves such as the Pixies (see page 58), would surface in her own work. In the early '90s, she formed the PJ Harvey Trio with drummer Rob Ellis and bassist Ian Oliver. The music of this period is loud, bluesy, and grungy. Her performance and the songs themselves were deliberately confrontational, often dealing with sexual politics and taboos (for example, "Happy and Bleeding"). Her second single "Sheela-Na-Gig," uses the metaphor of the Sheela na gig, a medieval carving of a naked woman with exaggerated sexual characteristics, to draw connections between misogyny, sexual squeamishness, and female self-loathing.

The trio pursued this style further on second album *Rid of Me* (1993), hiring Steve Albini to capture a raw, live sound (as Nirvana would do for *In Utero*). Around this time, I accidentally saw the PJ Harvey Trio supporting U2 at an enormous gig at Wembley Arena. (Don't be overly critical; I have a soft spot for '90s U2, and I was very young). I had little idea who she was, and most of the crowd had *no* idea who she was and didn't much care for her. I just remember that she looked tiny on the massive stage, dressed in black with only her guitar, but she made SO MUCH NOISE!

After this Harvey parted ways with the trio and embarked on one of her first artistic about-turns, recording *To Bring You My Love* (1995) with John Parish (who would be a frequent collaborator) and Bad Seed Mick Harvey (see page 96). The new material was still bluesy but, instead of being aggressive, it was sassy, sexy, and sinister with tremolo guitar and cheesy organs. "C'mon Billy" and "Down By The Water" are weird folk songs of sexual betrayal and infanticide, not unlike the murder ballads on which she would shortly sing with Nick Cave. The new material brought an image change as well. Harvey would perform in skimpy, brightly colored catsuits with thick, smeared makeup, a look that was at once sexy, vulnerable, and scary.

In 1996 she contributed to Nick Cave's *Murder Ballads* album (see page 96) and the two had a brief but tumultuous relationship. Harvey channeled some of this emotional trauma into *Is This Desire?* (1998), a more subtle, withdrawn record that dabbled with electronica. Its successor, *Stories from the City, Stories from the Sea* (2000), was a more conventionally arranged album of rock songs with folkish tinges, which won her the Mercury Music Prize. It featured a collaboration with Radiohead's Thom Yorke, "This Mess We're In", as well as glam stomper "This Is Love." 2004's *Uh Huh Her* was a bluesier affair that harked back to her first albums. Stripped back to voice, guitar, and percussion on all but a few songs, she played everything on the album apart from the drums.

Recent years have brought further stylistic about-turns. *White Chalk* (2007) was stripped back even further to Harvey's haunting voice and piano, augmented by a small selection of largely acoustic instruments. In 2011 she released *Let England Shake*, an album themed around present and historical conflicts (see below). It won her a second Mercury Prize. Her ninth album, *The Hope Six Demolition Project*, was released in April 2016. Harvey composed original music for Shane Meadows' harrowing TV drama *The Virtues*, broadcast in 2019.

TOP ALBUM *Let England Shake* (2011) This is an extraordinary album, the result of two years' research into historical and contemporary conflict. It draws on literary and artistic sources such as Harold Pinter and Goya, as well as the testimony of soldiers and contemporary conflict-survivors, but also manages to include a bleakly humorous reference to Eddie Cochran's intention to take his "Summertime Blues" to the United Nations. Sonically, it continues from the fragility of *White Chalk* but sounds even more skeletal, like rattled folk music unsteady on its feet. Harvey's voice sounds shrill, sometimes hysterical, and the ghosts of military bands drift across the landscape. If it's not too glib of me to say so, it sounds shell-shocked.

POP TRIVIA Harvey's latest album, *The Hope Six Demolition Project* (2016), was recorded under unusual circumstances. In early 2015 the former Inland Revenue gymnasium and rifle range at London's Somerset House was converted into a recording studio with one-way glass. Members of the public could pay for a 45-minute slot to watch Harvey and her musicians recording. Of course, you might get unlucky and witness a tea break.

JEFF BUCKLEY

Jeff Buckley had the voice of an angel and the face of a model. He seemed to absorb songs by osmosis and emit music like the rest of us emit CO_2.

Buckley was the son of troubled folk musician Tim Buckley, but reportedly only met him once. Raised by his mum and stepdad in California, Buckley worked for years as a session musician before heading to New York in 1990. There he found his own musical voice, playing gigs at small venues, in particular Sin-é in the East Village. Buckley's influences were diverse, taking in everything from Nina Simone and The Smiths (see page 46) to the Qawwali devotional music of Pakistani musician Nusrat Fateh Ali Khan. He played hundreds of cover versions, absorbing their styles into his own compositions, which he gradually added to his performances. By 1992 he had built a considerable following and signed to Columbia Records. He recruited a band and recorded his only studio album, *Grace*, inviting Gary Lucas to play guitar on "Mojo Pin" and "Grace," the songs that he co-wrote with him. The album was released in 1994 to critical acclaim but slow sales. Buckley spent the next two years touring the album all over the world. Hearing Buckley's swooping vocals in London in 1994 had a profound effect on Thom Yorke, inspiring a key stylistic breakthrough during the recording of *The Bends* (see page 94).

Preparations for album two, *My Sweetheart The Drunk,* were slow. Buckley and his band recorded three sessions with Television's Tom Verlaine as producer, but were dissatisfied with the results. Buckley asked Andy Wallace, who had produced *Grace*, to take over and began recording more demos for the upcoming session. On May 29, 1997, Buckley was on his way to the studio when he decided to go for a swim in Memphis' Wolf River and drowned, probably dragged under in the wake of a passing boat. What sticks in the craw beyond the tragic death of a young man is the loss of all that *potential*, of music that we'll never get to hear.

TOP ALBUM *Grace* (1994) From the mysterious fade-in of "Mojo Pin," this album has your attention. The swoop and soar of Buckley's voice, the intricate guitar motif of "Grace," the dynamic peaks and troughs, this is music that makes hairs stand on end. In addition to the original songs, *Grace* includes three covers— "Lilac Wine," the hymn "Corpus Christi Carol," and what, for many, is the definitive version of Leonard Cohen's "Hallelujah."

POP TRIVIA Since Buckley's death, a number of live recordings have been released, as well as *Sketches for My Sweetheart The Drunk* (1998), a collection of demos and work-in-progress for his second album. In 2016 *You And I* was also released, a collection of newly unearthed recordings from Buckley's first Colombia session.

PAVEMENT

Pavement were surrealist slackers from California, the Merry Pranksters of alternative music. Their records sound like Dada poetry set to stoner rock, giving stylistic nods to country and folk.

The band formed in 1989, initially as a recording project for Stephen Malkmus (vocals and guitar) and Scott Kannberg, aka Spiral Stairs (guitar). After releasing some EPs, the duo recruited a full band, with Mark Ibold on bass and Bob Nastanovich, whose roles included percussion, shouting, and helping first drummer, Gary Young, to keep time. The band's name hinted at Anglophile tastes (there ain't no pavements in California), particularly a love of The Fall (see page 48). Although sounding nothing like Mark E. Smith, Malkmus brought a similarly experimental approach to his lyrics, speak-singing strings of free-associated imagery. A noisy, lo-fi debut album *Slanted and Enchanted* came out in 1992. The song titles alone give you an idea of its cracked genius: "Zurich Is Stained," "Chesley's Little Wrists," "Jackals, False Grails: The Lonesome Era" anyone? I don't mind if I do.

Gary Young's behavior was too eccentric even for a band of eccentrics and he was dropped in favor of drummer Steve West. Their next record, *Crooked Rain, Crooked Rain* (1994), retained the word collage and scuzzy guitars, but mixed them with more accessible song structures and semi-coherent narratives. Catchy sing-along "Cut Your Hair" was an almost-hit for the band and second single "Gold Soundz" is a lovely skewed pop song. Next came the sprawling *Wowee Zowee* (1995), an 18-song tour de force of musical invention (see right). 1997's *Brighten The Corners* was an attempt to be more accessible. It contains some great songs, not least "Stereo,"

which hilariously wonders aloud about the speaking voice of Rush singer Geddy Lee, and "Shady Lane."

The band made one more album, but by this stage the fault lines were starting to show, particularly between Malkmus and Kannberg. After failing to produce their own record, they brought in Radiohead producer Nigel Godrich. The resulting album, *Terror Twilight* (1999), was composed entirely of Malkmus songs, a fact that only exacerbated tensions in the band. Regardless, it's one of the great last albums, up there with The Smiths' *Strangeways, Here We Come* (see page 46). It sounds more focused than previous albums, but still has some fantastic, lyrical non-sequiturs and moments of exquisite beauty. The band broke up messily and acrimoniously soon after. Malkmus has released nine albums since Pavement, solo and with his band The Jicks. In 2010 Pavement reformed and embarked on a world tour, but I didn't go to see them. I am an idiot.

TOP ALBUM *Wowee Zowee* (1995) This is brilliantly all over the place, exploring every musical idea and hitting upon some sublime moments in the process. It opens with the restrained shuffle of "We Dance" and Malkmus singing about castration. Funky jam "Rattled By The Rush" features some of the group's most inventive guitar playing, and the elegant "Father To A Sister Of Thought" boasts luscious table steel guitar.

POP TRIVIA The country-tinged "Range Life," from *Crooked Rain, Crooked Rain*, poked fun at The Smashing Pumpkins in its lyrics. Humorless rollercoaster-fan Billy Corgan took offence and had Pavement thrown off the 1994 Lollapalooza tour, which his band was headlining.

THE STONE ROSES

Along with the Happy Mondays, The Stone Roses were the swaggering kings of "Madchester," that pilled-up hybrid of guitar bands and club culture in Manchester in the late 1980s and early '90s.

For a band that made only two albums, their influence has been far-reaching. Their shuffling, "baggy" beat was all over everything in the early '90s (just listen to early Blur). In the longer term they reawakened an interest in the classic guitar bands of the '60s, which would eventually flower (or degrade, depending on your point of view) into Britpop.

Ian Brown (vocals) and John Squire (guitar) formed what would become The Stone Roses in 1983. Their sound developed gradually. 1987 single "Sally Cinnamon" never quite gets going, but has '60s chiming guitars and a lovely tune. Things really clicked when they recruited Gary "Mani" Mounfield as their new bassist. Mani and drummer Alan "Reni" Wren formed a formidable rhythm section, whose funky grooves underpinned The Stone Roses' best compositions. In 1989 they released their debut album, *The Stone Roses*, and its euphoric combination of classic pop hooks, jangly guitars, and funky workouts won them a new legion of fans. In May 1990 they played to 27,000 people at a concert in Spike Island, which has now assumed legendary proportions as THE seminal experience of the baggy generation.

Dissatisfied with their record company, Silvertone, the band tried to leave their contract and sign with Geffen. Thus began years of legal tussling and inactivity. By the time *Second Coming* (1994) was released, five long years later, the band's absence had assumed mythic proportions. There was no way this album could live up to the hype. Some liked it but many critics and fans found it underwhelming. Squire had largely taken over the songwriting reins, giving the album a bluesier, rockier sound than the debut. In truth, their moment had passed. Madchester was over and the band had drifted apart. Reni walked away in April 1995, soon followed by Squire. Brown and Mani soldiered on with new musicians before calling a halt in October 1996.

In 2011 the Roses reformed and in 2012 they toured the world, a period captured in Shane Meadows' fan documentary *The Stone Roses: Made of Stone* (2013). In May 2016 they debuted the singles "All For One" and "Beautiful Thing" but a hoped-for third album failed to materialize and in 2019 John Squire confirmed that the band had called it a day.

TOP ALBUM *The Stone Roses* (1989) I'll be honest, I'm not a huge fan. I think to really "get it" you needed to have been there at the time, but I'm slightly too young. There's some underwhelming filler on here—"Elizabeth My Dear" is just Scarborough Fair, isn't it—but it's also packed with storming indie classics: "She Bangs the Drums", "Waterfall", "This Is the One," and "I Am the Resurrection." For me, the album's strongest moments are its brooding, narcotic opener "I Wanna Be Adored" and the guaranteed floor-filler, "Fool's Gold."

POP TRIVIA Ian Brown may not be a great singer in the David Bowie sense of the word, but he has attitude in spades. He was apparently convinced to become a frontman during an encounter with legendary soul singer Geno Washington, (yes, he of Dexy's "Geno! Geno! Geno...!") who told him he would become a star.

Primal Scream

Primal Scream will forever be defined by their breakthrough album, *Screamadelica* (1991). Its hedonistic mingling of acid house and rock music fulfilled what The Stone Roses had hinted at, and Primal Scream became the band that brought dance music to the indie kids.

Bobby Gillespie (the only original member of the band) led Primal Scream through years of stylistic development before they reached their acid-house apotheosis in the early '90s. Their early recordings are in hoc to the jangly '60s rock of The Byrds and to Scottish '80s indie pop like Orange Juice. Early fan-favorite "Velocity Girl" sounds almost exactly like an average Stone Roses song. Reduced to a core group of Gillespie, Andrew Innes, and Robert "Throb" Young, they embraced garage rock for 1989's *Primal Scream*, looking back to The Stooges (see page 18) and MC5, by way of The Jesus and Mary Chain (see page 53). Though this album failed to make much of an impact, it did produce the song that eventually led to their breakthrough moment.

Introduced to the acid house scene by Creation Record's boss Alan McGee, the band asked DJ Andrew Weatherall to remix the Stones-esque song "I'm Losing More Than I'll Ever Have" from their latest album. He responded by ditching most of the song (including the vocal), looping the original song's bluesy closing refrain, and adding sampled drums, gospel vocals, and footage from the Peter Fonda movie *The Wild Angels*. The resulting collage was "Loaded," the band's first hit and the song that announced them as groovy, iconoclastic hedonists. On *Screamadelica* the band continued with this mixture of gospel-tinged rock and club beats. The album was a huge hit in the UK, producing crossover classics "Movin' On Up" and "Come Together," as well as genuine club bangers like "Higher Than The Sun."

For their follow-up, the band returned to their love of garage and blues-rock. *Give Out But Don't Give Up* (1994) allowed Gillespie to indulge his fantasy of being Mick Jagger and is something of a return to the sound of *Primal Scream* (except better). It produced the sing-along hit single "Rocks," although some critics and fans were confused that such an innovative band had returned to such a retro, imitative sound. The band took a more experimental turn again with 1997's *Vanishing Point*, stirring paranoid dub and psychedelic Krautrock into the mix. They pushed this sound further with 1999's scarily dystopian *XTRMNTR* (see right) and on subsequent albums have veered between their blues-rock comfort zone and weirder electronic experiments.

Beneath all the stylistic changes, at the heart of Primal Scream lies a curiously old-fashioned belief in the redemptive and rebellious spirit of rock 'n' roll. Bobby Gillespie is a great rock frontman in the vein of Jagger, and in the '90s the notoriously hedonistic band seemed to live in a private '70s time capsule. Sometimes, though, the constant call-backs to classic rock icons are a little wearing. Yes, we get that Lee Hazlewood and Nancy Sinatra were cool, but do you have to sing their song with Kate flipping Moss?

"Throb" Young died in 2014 and game-changing remixer Andrew Weatherall died in 2020.

TOP ALBUM *XTRMNTR* (2000) The opening song is called "Kill All Hippies," but maybe this should be "Kill All Vowels." *Screamadelica* is great, but occasionally you need something with a bit more grit. Frankly, "Accelerator" sounds f***ing terrifying, with relentless walls of guitar turned up to 13, like the MC5 put through a particle accelerator. "Exterminator" and "Swastika Eyes" are all atonal electro-Krautrock, like sped-up footage of a car journey through a post-apocalyptic landscape. Gillespie lazily drawls lyrical venom on the newly minted 21st century, intoning "civil disobedience" and diagnosing "a military-industrial illusion of democracy." It's bracing stuff, and there's no Kate Moss in sight.

POP TRIVIA Apart from a core group of Gillespie, Innes, and keyboard player, Martin Duffy, an impressive array of musicians have drifted in and out of Primal Scream over the years. Mani played bass for the group between the breakup and eventual reformation of The Stone Roses. Since *XTRMNTR*, Kevin Shields (of My Bloody Valentine) has been a semi-regular member of the band. During *Screamadelica* and *Give Out But Don't Give Up*, the band featured additional vocals from Denise Johnson.

RADIOHEAD

Radiohead have a justly miserablist reputation. In the 1990s they were the kings of "complaint rock" (a phrase coined by that barometer of a generation, Cher from 1995's cult comedy *Clueless*) and have evolved into cranky, experimental refuseniks and apocalyptic doomsayers.

Thom Yorke, brothers Johnny and Colin Greenwood, Ed O'Brien, and Phil Selway formed the dreadfully named band On A Friday at school in Oxfordshire in the mid-1980s. They signed to EMI in the early '90s and renamed themselves after the Talking Heads' song "Radio Head" (see page 35). They were always more interested in US bands than British ones, and in the long run their status as outsiders in their own country allowed them to sidestep the treacherous bog of Britpop. They absorbed the dynamic range and guitar-mangling tricks of their beloved Pixies (see page 58) and by the time of their debut album, *Pablo Honey* (1993), they sounded like the British equivalent of grunge. The album and its single "Creep" initially stalled in the UK, but after becoming popular on US College Radio, and then receiving extensive play on MTV, "Creep" was re-released to much greater attention at home. Still, the song, with its heartfelt expression of outsiderdom/petulant moaning, became something of a millstone for the band.

They set out to prove themselves by recording their second album with UK indie veteran John Leckie. The first fruit of this session was 1995's *My Iron Lung* EP. The song's central metaphor of the iron lung as something that sustains and constricts was a self-savaging reaction to the success of "Creep." The song musically quoted Nirvana's "Heart-Shaped Box," while Yorke sang deadpan about corporate rock repetition. The revelation of the EP was not only that the A-side was brilliant, and more adventurous and complex than anything from *Pablo Honey*, but that the six other songs were just as good. I recall listening to the EP with friends and it dawning on us that they weren't one-hit-wonders after all. *The Bends* (1995) did not disappoint. The band, and Yorke in particular, had developed into versatile songwriters. "High and Dry" and "Fake Plastic Trees" were emotionally bruised ballads that built into rockers, while the title track and "Just" were thrilling duels of amped-up guitars. What really stood out were Yorke's soaring voice, reminiscent in places of Jeff Buckley (see page 90), and Johnny Greenwood's crookedly expressive guitar lines. *My Iron Lung* and *The Bends* also marked the beginnings of the band's relationship with two key collaborators: Stanley Donwood and Nigel Godrich. Donwood designed the often sarcastic and terrifying artwork that would be a key part of every Radiohead release, marketing campaign, and website henceforth. Godrich, who became Radiohead's equivalent of The Beatles' George Martin, was the engineer for these sessions.

Godrich ascended to the producer's chair for the band's follow-up album, *OK Computer* (1997). "Airbag" shows the influence of DJ Shadow (see page 82), its weird, dubby bass dropping in, then cutting out with the syncopated drums. *OK Computer* pushed further into the terrain mapped out by *The Bends*, building extended and experimental song structures (see the bolted-together, six-and-a-half-minute single "Paranoid Android") out of complex guitar arrangements. It also contained "Lucky," maybe the most beautiful and optimistic song they ever managed. (Amazingly, this song was Godrich's first production duty for the band and was recorded in five hours. Not bad for a day's work, lads!) Lyrically, the album's themes are all millennial angst and cultural dislocation caused by information overload. These themes were emphasized by Donwood's artwork, which spoofed safety announcements and self-help manuals. "Fitter Happier" is a creepy monolog, assembled from context-less self-help platitudes, like being stuck in a nightmarish pep talk with Stephen Hawking. For such a pessimistic and experimental album, *OK Computer* proved remarkably popular. It's the last Radiohead album that everyone under 40 has heard and is considered one of their most accessible records (cause, y'know, it's still got guitars). The 1999 documentary *Meeting People is Easy* shows the band touring the world and struggling to come to terms with their fame. Yorke and co. spent the next 20 years running away from mainstream success.

The retreat began in earnest with *Kid A* (2000) and *Amnesiac* (2001) (see right). In the time since *OK Computer*, the band—and Yorke in particular—had become obsessed with electronic musicians such as Warp Records artists Aphex Twin (see page 99) and Autechre. Much of *Kid A* eschewed conventional song structures for electronic loops and programming, and experimented with digitally distorting Yorke's voice. Lyrically, the band's new material was less personal and more focused on global warnings of political and environmental breakdown. If the band's subjects were bigger, they were also perversely more opaque, the lyrics fractured into ill-fitting pieces. This was partly a method for Yorke to defeat his writer's block. There are still guitars on *Kid A* and *Amnesiac* but you wouldn't know it from the reaction. Both albums split public and critical opinion.

In 2003 Radiohead released *Hail To The Thief*, a record that more consciously mixed their rock-with-guitars and electronic-experimental tendencies. Its lyrics are full of invective and resentment, and the album's title makes it clear that no small part of its rage was aimed at George W. Bush, Tony Blair, and the "War on Terror." Yorke continued down this more explicitly political path on his solo album, *The Eraser* (2006), which featured a song about the UK weapons expert David Kelly.

Having fulfilled their contract with EMI, the band decided to go it alone and found themselves, as *The New York Times* wrote, "by far the world's most popular unsigned band." In 2007, with little notice, they self-released *In Rainbows* through their website as a download, on a pay-what-you-want basis, including £0. They were the first major band to release an album in this way and it was reportedly downloaded over a million times on the first day of its release, although, as media

there there X

observers wryly noted, this was a band who had enjoyed the benefit of the EMI marketing machine for over 10 years. What got a little lost in the hype and debates about the decline of the record industry was that *In Rainbows* is a beautiful record, full of moody shade and light, from the surprisingly funky opener "15 Step," to the Nick Drake-esque "Faust Arp," to the laid-back (and actually a bit sexy?!) "House of Cards." In 2011 they self-released another album, *The King of Limbs*, a sketchier record of trip-hoppy, glitchy electronica, and in May 2016 they released their ninth album, the spooky and beautiful *A Moon Shaped Pool*, complete with its 'Trumpton does the Wicker Man' video for lead single "Burn the Witch." In 2019 a hacker attempted to hold the band hostage by threatening to release several hours of work-in-progress from the *OK Computer* sessions. They responded savvily by selling the material online, with all proceeds given to Exctinction Rebellion.

TOP ALBUMS *Kid A* (2000) and *Amnesiac* (2001) It's a bit of a cheat, but I'm going to have two albums, as they were both compiled from the same sessions. Don't be scared of these electronic siblings; they're not *that* weird, it's just that they wrong-footed everyone at the time. *Kid A* is my favorite Radiohead album, despite strong contention from *In Rainbows*. It opens with trippy and hilarious "Everything In Its Right Place"—

just a keyboard, Yorke, and a set of mutating digital clones. "Kid A," the song, sounds like a robotic music box having a nervous breakdown and then it's on to the mighty "The National Anthem," in which a big, dumb, distorted bassline is augmented by a skronking jazz orchestra inspired by Charlie Mingus. *Amnesiac* isn't quite as much fun, but does contain the beautiful "Pyramid Song" (I *still* can't work out what time signature it's in!) and Thom Yorke singing backward on "Like Spinning Plates." It also features the late great jazz trumpeter and comedy presenter Humphrey Lyttelton on album closer "Life In A Glasshouse."

POP TRIVIA The band members have notched up an impressive range of extra-curricular activities. Yorke has released three solo albums, scored horror remake *Suspiria* and formed a band, Atoms for Peace, with Godrich and Flea from the Red Hot Chili Peppers. Drummer Phil Selway has released two solo albums and dabbled with radio presenting for BBC 6 Music. Ed O'Brien, trading as EOB, released his debut solo album in 2020. Johnny Greenwood has carved out a formidable reputation as a composer of film scores, notably for the films of Paul Thomas Anderson. Anderson also directed the Netflix short for Yorke's 2019 album *Anima*.

NICK CAVE AND THE BAD SEEDS

Sunny Australia was never going to hold Nick Cave for too long. It was in Britain that he found a setting that was more suited to his gothic temperament. Cave has long been a refreshing counterpoint to more pedestrian "alternative" bands, weaving tales of murder and religious damnation.

Cave's first band The Birthday Party were gothic post-punks, who were notorious for their confrontational and violent live shows. After dissolving the band (presumably in holy water), he recruited a new backing band, initially incorporating fellow Birthday Party alumnus Mick Harvey and Blixa Bargeld of industrial band Einstürzende Neubaten. Nick Cave and The Bad Seeds released their first album, *From Her To Eternity*, in 1984. Cave continued with the melodramatic delivery he developed in his first band and further indulged his taste for American gothic and Old Testament damnation. But the new band pulled away from the antagonistic noise-rock of The Birthday Party in favor of a stripped-back, menacing blues-rock. They pursued this vision of American gothic blues on 1985's *The Firstborn Is Dead*, whose title alludes to Elvis Presley's stillborn twin. On the covers album *Kicking Against The Pricks* (1986), Cave paid tribute to his influences, including Johnny Cash, John Lee Hooker, and traditional American gospel.

The band's popularity grew over their next two albums. *Your Funeral... My Trial* (1986) bears the influence of Tom Waits (see page 26), particularly on the nightmarish short story "The Carny." *Tender Prey* (1988) featured death row ballad "The Mercy Seat," later covered by Johnny Cash. After a stint in rehab Cave moved to Brazil, where he fell in love and married. The mellower tone of *The Good Son* (1990) nonplussed fans at the time, who expected more tales of gothic excess. In retrospect, the album is the first intimation of one of the strongest suits of Cave's later songwriting: his brooding, emotional piano ballads. "The Weeping Song" and "The Ship Song" are both mainstays of The Bad Seeds' repertoire to this day. The fans needn't have worried, as things got noisy and scabrous again on the next record, *Henry's Dream* (1992).

Cave and co. began a period of critical acclaim and popularity with *Let Love In* (1994), a masterpiece of taut menace and occasional furious outbursts. Highlights included "Do You Love Me?" and "Red Right Hand," which would go on to be one of their most popular songs. 1996's *Murder Ballads* upped the blood and guts to absurd levels, resulting in an album that is as funny as it is horrible (check out "Stagger Lee" for some seriously nasty lyrics). At this point, Cave was a fascinating, ghoulish figure, haunting the fringes of the mainstream with his Kylie duet "Where The Wild Roses Go." He was an unwelcome guest at the Britpop backslapping feast, telling lurid tales of serial killers and sociopaths. The end of Cave's marriage and a brief relationship with PJ Harvey, with whom he had dueted on *Murder Ballads,* colored his subsequent album, *The Boatman's Call* (1997). Its songs, notably "Into My Arms" and "West Country Girl," are in the tradition of hymns and folk songs, stately odes to regret and loss.

Nick Cave and The Bad Seeds have released seven albums since, including the double album *Abattoir Blues/The Lyre of Orpheus* (2004) and *Dig, Lazarus, Dig!!!* (2008). *Push The Sky Away* (2013) was a downbeat minimalist record with Cave's crooned observations supported by sketchy guitars and noodly loops. *Skeleton Tree* (2016) was haunted by the tragic death of Cave's teenage son, Arthur, although most of the album had been written before this event. Grief and love are among the meaty themes explored on the beautiful and spectral album *Ghosteen*, released in 2019. In 2007 Cave formed new group Grinderman, confusingly/mischievously composed of much the same line-up as the Bad Seeds—Warren Ellis, Martyn P. Casey, and Jim Sclavunos. This "new" band focused on the messier, more raucous side of things. Grinderman's eponymous first album (2007) was a loose (and frequently hilarious) concept album about middle-aged lust. Cave grew a splendid moustache to mark the occasion.

TOP ALBUMS *Abattoir Blues/The Lyre of Orpheus* (2004) Take two of Nick Cave's best albums into the listening booth? No need, when you can listen to this double album. Guaranteed, absolutely no filler, or I'm an Aussie vampire bat. The first record has the rockier numbers and proves that Cave sounds even better with a gospel choir behind him. "There She Goes, My Beautiful World" includes descriptions of Karl Marx's carbuncles and the habits of the literary greats. *The Lyre of Orpheus* contains the gentler, more romantic stuff, but the gospel choir sneak back in for epic album closer "O Children."

POP TRIVIA Cave has written two novels and an introduction to an edition of Mark's Gospel, as well as screenplays for *The Proposition* and *Lawless*. Recently he has pioneered direct contact with fans online in The Red Hand Files, periodically answering questions posted on the website in a series of frank missives dealing with creativity, art and politics, and offering advice like your cool, gothic uncle..

the chemical brothers

Ed Simons and Tom Rowlands, aka The Chemical Brothers, are dance music pioneers from the UK, known for their aggressive, punchy take on big beat and a taste for psychedelia. In the 1990s they achieved popularity alongside Britpop bands and became the favorite dance act of alt-rock fans.

The Chemical Brothers formed in Manchester where they were both students. They received early support from DJ Andrew Weatherall and debut album *Exit Planet Dust* (1995) was jointly released in the UK by their Freestyle Dust label and Weatherall's Junior Boy's Own. *Exit Planet Dust* established their taste for fast, hard-hitting beats and featured vocal cameos from Beth Orton ("Alive Alone") and The Charlatans' Tim Burgess ("Life Is Sweet").

Their reputation as the dance act that rock fans liked was confirmed when they supported Oasis (see page 86) at Knebworth in 1997. Noel Gallagher then guested on their Number One single, "Setting Sun," which was included on their next album *Dig Your Own Hole* (1997). 1999's *Surrender* had a more house-influenced sound and featured the hit single "Hey Boy Hey Girl," as well as more collaborations from indie's great and good. Noel Gallagher sang on that other trippy number "Let Forever Be," while Bernard Sumner (see page 50) and Bobby Gillespie (see page 93) teamed up for "Out of Control." The Chemical Brothers repaid the favor to Gillespie by contributing production to Primal Scream's "Swastika Eyes" on *XTRMNTR* (2000).

The Chemical Brothers have since released five studio albums, notably 2005's hip-hop-inflected *Push The Button* (2005), which includes the single "Galvanise," featuring Q-Tip. They have continued their practice of collaborating with guest vocalists, although 2010's *Further* was something of a reaction against this, opting for a less starry, more self-enclosed atmosphere. In 2012 they composed an official song for the London Olympics cycling events. "Theme for Velodrome" was an orchestral trance number with a robot voice that tipped its cycling helmet toward Kraftwerk (see page 38). *Born in the Echoes* (2015) again featured Q-Tip on robot-rock-rap number "Go" and St. Vincent (see page 150) on eerie "Under Neon Lights." In 2019 they released their ninth studio album, *No Geography*.

TOP ALBUM *Dig Your Own Hole* (1997) This is perhaps their most diverse and satisfying record. "Block Rockin' Beats" is irresistible and does just what it says on the tin, while "Dig Your Own Hole" and "Get Up On It Like This" are exercises in manic funk. "Setting Sun" is arguably Noel Gallagher's best song. It owes a heavy debt to The Beatles' "Tomorrow Never Knows," but it takes the Fab Four somewhere new—namely to a rave.

POP TRIVIA Starting out as club DJs in Manchester in the early '90s, The Chemical Brothers took inspiration from their heroes the Dust Brothers and named themselves... the Dust Brothers. Great idea, lads! When they started getting popular, the (original) Dust Brothers weren't best pleased, necessitating a hasty name change to The Chemical Brothers.

APHEX TWIN

Richard James, better known as Aphex Twin, is an influential pioneer of electronic music. He's particularly associated with Warp Records, but released early material on a bewildering range of independent labels and under a bewildering range of pseudonyms.

James' first album, *Selected Ambient Works 85–92* (1992), developed Brian Eno's notion of ambient music, creating tracks defined by gently pulsing basslines and hypnagogic beats. Its sequel, *Selected Ambient Works Volume II* (1994), began his association with Warp. The tracks on this album were more mysterious, with less reliance on rhythm and melody. Later releases returned to an interest in rhythm, influenced by jungle and drum and bass. *...I Care Because You Do* (1995) mixed atmospheric soundscapes with percussive tracks and *Richard D. James Album* (1996) featured faster, manic tempos influenced by James' friend Luke Vibert. These albums also established Aphex Twin's habit of adorning his records with his own face, a reaction against the anonymizing nature of dance music. He extended this provocative playing with his own image into the packaging and video of the *Come to Daddy* EP (1997), both of which featured depictions of schoolchildren, all with James' identical face. The terrifying video and uncharacteristically loud, atonal track made Aphex Twin briefly notorious. The video and sleeve for "Windowlicker" repeated the trick two years later, mocking hyper-sexualized hip-hop imagery by putting James' grinning, demonic face on a bikini-clad beach beauty.

In 2001, Warp released his last album for 14 years. *Drukqs*, a diverse double album featuring computer-controlled piano, divided critical opinion. While on apparent hiatus, he kept busy releasing experimental material on his own Rephlex Records label and recording under a variety of new aliases. In 2014 Warp released his long-awaited album *Syro*. A handful of EPs, videos, and limited edition pressings have followed in the years since. When asked for a description of his musical style, James has rejected the label IDM (Intelligent Dance Music). His Rephlex Records label has suggested the lovely term: "braindance."

TOP ALBUM *Selected Ambient Works Volume II* (1994) This pursued ambient music further into abstraction, jettisoning melody in favor of repeated patterns of sound and gradually developing tones. James later said that these compositions were inspired by lucid dreaming and his experiences of synesthesia. The mysterious nature of the compositions was reflected in the album's packaging. The tracks were not given names, but could be matched with corresponding pictures of natural and man-made materials. If push came to shove, I'd say my favorite track is "#6 (Mold)."

POP TRIVIA The infamous videos for "Come to Daddy" and "Windowlicker" were directed by Chris Cunningham, who first tried out his "multiple faces" idea on the inside sleeve of The Auteurs' *After Murder Park* (1996), replacing the faces of schoolchildren with that of misanthropic singer Luke Haines. He also directed the video for Björk's "All is Love," in which two Björk-faced robots make love.

daft punk

This book is full of punk bands who sound nothing like punk, so it should come as no surprise that Daft Punk sound nothing like their name suggests. They are famous as the chart-topping French robots who combine house music with ear-worm repetitive melodies. What they do perhaps have in common with punk is a spirit of self-reliance and independence.

The name for the band came originally from a bad review in UK music paper *Melody Maker*, which described their previous band Darlin' as "a daft punky thrash." After Darlin' broke up, Thomas Bangalter and Guy-Manuel de Homem-Christo turned their backs on guitar music and embraced dance and the possibilities of electronic composition. Their first single, the monstrously catchy "Da Funk," was unleashed upon the world in 1997. With a major hit on their hands (still human at this point), they devoted their energies to recording an album. *Homework* came out in 1997 and did brisk business, assisted by memorable videos directed by Spike Jonze, Michel Gondry, and Roman Coppola. Jonze's video for "Da Funk" featured Charles, a hapless anthropomorphic dog with a crutch, hobbling through a series of humdrum encounters in New York. Daft Punk directed a sequel video for "Fresh," which showed Charles in happier climes.

Discovery (2001) had a more synthy, Europop feel than its predecessor. As "Da Funk" had done for *Homework*, so "One More Time" did for *Discovery*, promoting its parent album and establishing the band's new dominant style of vocoder vocals over ultra-compressed music. Seeking to build upon the videos from their first album, the group commissioned Kazuhisa Takenouchi to direct a Japanese-French sci-fi anime film with *Homework* as its soundtrack. This was also the period when Bangalter and de Homem-Christo began wearing helmets and gloves to give them the appearance of robots.

They played on this notion of them as musical androids on 2005's *Human After All*. The album wasn't as well received as its predecessors, but produced a hit single in "Robot Rock," which, as its title suggests, does indeed rock. Next, Daft Punk directed and released their own film, *Electroma* (2006), which perversely features none of their music. This strange rejig of *Frankenstein* depicts the two Daft Punk robots trying to become human and being ostracized by their fellow robots as a consequence. Daft Punk scored the 2010 movie *Tron: Legacy* before beginning work on their next album, *Random Access Memories* (2013).

As before, they built up public appetite for the album with a catchy single, but this one ascended to a new level of popularity altogether. "Get Lucky," co-written and performed with Nile Rodgers (see page 31) and off-duty mountie Pharrell Williams, became the monster hit of 2013. The album paid lavish tribute to the disco and dance pioneers of the '70s and '80s. In addition to Rodgers and Williams, it featured collaborations with Giorgio Moroder, Chilly Gonzales, Julian Casablancas of The Strokes (see page 112), and Panda Bear of Animal Collective (see page 133). It's a weird album, definitely a collection of *songs* as opposed to *tracks*, in a way that even *Discovery* wasn't, and it's undeniably an impressive achievement. The trouble is, it sounds so lush and does such a convincing job of aping the era it venerates, that you wonder a little bit what the point is. You might as well go and listen to The Doobie Brothers, or indeed Chic (see page 31). "Get Lucky" is great, though.

TOP ALBUM *Discovery* (2001) This album takes the template established on *Homework* (1997), but adds a more personal dimension with the frequent vocoder vocals. The tracks are more recognizably *songs* than on the debut, with chord changes, bridge sections, and electronically treated guitar livening the mix. You can imagine actual robots writing songs like "Digital Love," trying to pass a songwriters' version of the Turing Test. The second half of "Short Circuit" sounds like a hung-over robot with a sore head, berating himself for some digital misdemeanor the night before. I find this far more moving than anything on *Random Access Memories*.

POP TRIVIA Daft Punk's robot schtick obviously owes quite a lot to Kraftwerk (as does their music), but whereas Kraftwerk modeled creepy automata on the actual members of the band, Daft Punk have used their robot personas to achieve anonymity. Before they settled on their robot identities, Bangalter and de Homem-Christo would often wear other masks or hide their faces in interviews. The irony is that in finding such an effective means of hiding, they have created an instantly recognizable mega-brand. Since *Discovery* (2001), they have modified the designs of their robot heads for each release. There are, of course, pictures of Bangalter and de Homem-Christo on the Internet sans masks. They look, surprise surprise, like men from France.

BECK

For a spell in the 1990s it looked like Beck was about to achieve a kind of musical Glasnost, pulling down all stylistic barriers by making music that was simultaneously *every* genre—hip-hop, country, grunge, blues, soul, funk, folk...

Beck Hansen grew up in LA in the '70s and '80s, busking and playing low-key gigs as a blues and alt-folk musician before stumbling upon a hit with his slacker-anthem "Loser" in 1993. "Loser" is like the fun version of Radiohead's "Creep," channeling its self-hating spirit through blues guitar, sitar, and a shuffling hip-hop beat. Like Radiohead, Beck found himself labeled a one-hit wonder. "Loser" was included on the experimental grungy album *Mellow Gold* (1994), but he would have to wait until 1996's *Odelay* to really prove his mettle. *Odelay* is a genre-busting, era-defining work of genius that managed to combine radical stylistic mash-ups with direct pop appeal. It's no accident that this "Frankenstein's masterpiece" was produced by the Dust Brothers, who had also facilitated the Beastie Boys' sample-rich breakthrough, *Paul's Boutique* (see page 66). This stitched-together aesthetic is also reflected in Beck's lyrics, which are surreal accretions of dislocated imagery, somewhat reminiscent of Pavement's Stephen Malkmus (see page 91). *Odelay* is stuffed to its eclectic gills with modern alternative classics: "Devil's Haircut," "The New Pollution," "Where It's At," and "Jack-Ass."

Beck recruited Nigel Godrich (fresh from the release of Radiohead's *OK Computer*) to produce a more low-key album. *Mutations* (1998) was recorded quickly and intended to reflect the sound of Beck and his band live. It emphasized the country and folk elements in his sound, but managed still to be diverse and inventive, demonstrating that Beck didn't *need* to rely on samples and sound collages.

The big-budget follow-up to *Odelay* was 1999's *Midnite Vultures*, which mixed new flavors into Beck's sonic gumbo, notably Stax-era soul and George Clinton funk (see page 36). He made another stylistic U-turn in 2002 with *Sea Change*, an album of beautiful and desolate heartbreak, ruminating on the split from his long-term girlfriend. The really radical thing about *Sea Change* was how straight it sounded, both in its earnest country-folk sound and direct, unaffected lyrics. "Paper Tiger" featured an arrangement inspired by Serge Gainsbourg, whose daughter, Charlotte, Beck would go on to act as producer for.

Over the following years Beck continued to mix up musical styles and production approaches, although rarely to the same dazzling effect as on *Odelay*. 2005's *Guero* brought the Dust Brothers back into the fold. "Güero" is Mexican slang for "white boy" or "blondey," a catcall Beck had often heard while growing up in the Hispanic parts of LA. The album duly leaned toward Latin American music, in particular Brazilian samba, and featured samples of Spanish-spoken street slang. Beck had been working concurrently on another album with Godrich, which became *The Information* (2006). He enlisted Danger Mouse to produce his 2008 album *Modern Guilt*, which had a '60s psychedelic vibe.

In 2014 he released *Morning Phase,* a belated follow-up to *Sea Change* (2002). Partially recorded at Jack White's Third

Man Records studio in Nashville (see page 114), it enlisted many of the same musicians as the earlier record and returned to *Sea Change*'s territory of country- and folk-rock. *Morning Phase* won Beck three Grammys in 2015, which inspired Kanye West to get up on the stage and look angry. Beck headed back towards planet Pop for 2017's extremely danceable *Colors*. His latest album, *Hyperspace* (2019) is an electro-soul collaboration with Pharrell Williams. He doesn't stand still for long, our Beck.

TOP ALBUM *Midnite Vultures* (1999) On this album a baby-faced Beck reinvents himself as an unlikely sex symbol. The album is, at least on one level, an hour-long, affectionately demented impression of Prince (see page 60). The tunes are plastic-soul jams with processed horns and digital squelches, and the normally plain-singing Beck finds within him an impressive falsetto. His surreal lyrics take on a newly libidinous urge, hinting at a new form of sex filthier than anyone had previously imagined. "Milk and Honey" features guest guitar from Johnny Marr (see page 46) and "Sexx Laws" has a mean banjo solo.

POP TRIVIA Preoccupied by the idea of jazz standards and Broadway songs composed before "definitive" recorded versions were the norm, Beck released *Song Reader* (2012) as a book of sheet music, inviting fans to perform, interpret, and record the new material themselves. We bought *Song Reader* as a present for my brother-in-law, but we still haven't been invited round for a performance. Beck did eventually release an audio album of *Song Reader,* featuring live versions played by other musicians.

BECK'S free association comic strip

Belle and Sebastian

Look at Belle and Sebastian's artful, monochrome record sleeves. Remind you of anyone? Yes, it's The Smiths. Belle and Sebastian are the band who thought that early Morrissey was just too macho and decided to out-fey the Manchester legends.

Whereas The Smiths' record covers were taken from Morrissey's favorite films, Belle and Sebastian's artwork features friends of the band. This reflects something of the band's music. It might be fragile, winsome melancholy, but it's a DIY, homemade melancholy. The early albums sound charmingly rough around the edges, seemingly recorded in a school hall as an art project by a bunch of friends.

The band had indeed started as a sort of school project (albeit Stuart Murdoch was 28 at the time)—debut album *Tigermilk* (1996) was recorded and released as part of a Music Business course at Stow College in Glasgow, Scotland. Stuart Murdoch had dropped out of university in his early twenties with ME and, while convalescing, had started to write songs, weaving stories out of his memories and the minutiae of life. Like early Morrissey, his lyrical voice came from this sense of seclusion, an outsider-status caused by years of staying inside. B&S followed *Tigermilk* with their classic album *If You're Feeling Sinister* (1996) and a string of great EPs, including *Lazy Line Painter Jane* (later collected on *Push Barman To Open Old Wounds* in 2005). At this time they were the great oddball indie band of their era,

releasing records at their own pace, missives from an apparent world of duffel coats, sexual confusion, and rummage sales.

Although the band co-produced their early albums with Tony Duggan, they hired 80s' super-producer Trevor Horn for 2003's *Dear Catastrophe Waitress*. They have since moved away from the "satchels and corduroys" fey sound of their early albums. *Girls in Peacetime Want to Dance* (2015), incorporates funky bass, samba drums, and dance programming. In 2018 they released three EPs, collectively titled (tongue in cheek) *How to Solve Our Human Problems* and in 2019 a soundtrack album for the film *Days of the Bagnold Summer* (starring Nick Cave's son, Earl).

TOP ALBUM *Fold Your Hands Child, You Walk Like a Peasant* (2000) Conventional wisdom states that this is the album where the band overstretched themselves. Well, I'm not having that—it's a masterpiece of baroque pop. Listen to the soaring strings of "I Fought In A War," the rambling harpsichord of "The Model," the creepy, backward-country of "Beyond The Sunrise," and the Beach-Boys-on-valium vibe of "Nice Day For A Sulk." On "Women's Realm" they become the great white soul band that Scotland never knew it needed.

POP TRIVIA The 1998 album and song *The Boy With The Arab Strap* was named after fellow Scots, Arab Strap, with whom B&S had toured. Murdoch has since said that he had no idea at the time that an Arab Strap is a sexual aid.

SUPER FURRY ANIMALS

Have there ever been better lyrics written than this?

Hermann loves Pauline and Pauline loves Hermann.
They made love and gave birth to a little German.
They call him MC^2 because he raps like no other,
An asthma sufferer like Ernesto Guevara.

Were they only to have given us this song about Einstein and his parents ("Hermann Loves Pauline" from 1996's *Radiator*) that would already be plenty, but the Super Furry Animals (SFA) have given us (thus far) nine albums of experimental, witty, psychedelic rock in English and Welsh.

Formed in Cardiff in 1993, the group have rarely stood still since. Their rambunctious debut *Fuzzy Logic* (1996) was associated with the fag end of Britpop, but SFA were both *too* Welsh for that London-centric scene and *too* inventive. *Radiator* (1997) moved beyond the cod-psychedelia of their debut, creating songs that were sharper and more sonically adventurous. The next album, *Guerilla*, was simultaneously catchy and experimental, featuring ear-worm melodies put through discombobulating aural mangles.

In 2000, SFA self-released their Welsh-language album *Mwng*, a beautiful collection of songs in their native tongue. The band turned about-face again for the glossy, sonically busy *Rings Around the World* (2001), a not-quite-a-concept-album released on DVD with a lavish set of music videos. Their last album, 2009's *Dark Days/Light Years* was a typically eclectic affair, including German rapping on "Inaugural Trams" by Franz Ferdinand's Nick McCarthy (see page 119). After going on hiatus in 2010 the band members have started various projects, and Gruff Rhys' solo efforts have been particularly diverse. In 2014 he released a record, film, book, and app called *American Interior*, a musical investigation of John Evans, an 18th-century Welshman in search of a tribe of Welsh-speaking Native Americans. He has put out two solo albums since, the orchestral *Babelsberg* (2018) and 2019's Welsh-language *Pang!* Rhys' melodious singing style is matched by his warm but slowww manner when speaking. Seriously, he seems to be living at half speed, like a giant tortoise. How does he get all this work done? Still, I hope that he lives to be 120.

TOP ALBUM *Guerilla* (1999) This was intended to be SFA's big pop record, but it's a brave, adventurous version of pop. "Wherever I Lay My Phone (That's My Home)" sounds like Gruff is off his nut with the chipmunks in a techno club, and "Some Things Come From Nothing" is a beautiful zen puzzle set to ambient music.

POP TRIVIA SFA's strong visual identity is, to a large extent, down to Welsh illustrator Pete Fowler, who has designed their sleeves, t-shirts, posters, videos, guitars, and giant inflatables since 1997's *Radiator*. Before bringing Fowler on board, the band's best marketing strategy was to convert a tank into a soundsystem.

APOLOGIES TO PETE FOWLER

★★★★★ CHAPTER FOUR ★★★★★

THE Millennium STAGE

★★★★★ ★★★★★ ★★★★★ ★★★★★

FEATURING THE FOLLOWING ARTISTS:

★★★★★ ★★★★★ ★★★★★ ★★★★★

Sufjan Stevens
lcd soundsystem
The Flaming Lips
HOT CHIP
QUEENS OF THE STONE AGE
AMY WINEHOUSE
TV ON THE RADIO
FLEET FOXES
The Strokes
elbow
JOANNA NEWSOM
THE WHITE STRIPES
KANYE WEST
ARCADE FIRE
Goldfrapp
wilco
ANIMAL COLLECTIVE
Franz Ferdinand
THE XX
OUTKAST
ARCTIC MONKEYS
DIZZEE RASCAL

★ INDIE ★ EXPERIMENTAL ★ SOUL ★ ELECTRONICA ★
HIP-HOP ★ FOLK ★ ROCK ★ GRIME

Sufjan Stevens

With his penchant for a bizarre project, Sufjan Stevens is my favorite musician of the 21st century. He makes music in a dizzying variety of styles, from folk to baroque pop to all-out electro weirdness.

Stevens' Christian beliefs have been a constant presence in his music and occasionally a more explicit theme, as on 2004's *Seven Swans*. But his religion rarely causes him to be preachy, functioning more as a cultural scaffold for his metaphysical ponderings, leading him into self-doubt and pain as much as solace.

In 2003 Stevens announced that he would record a concept album about each of the 50 US states. In fact, he only recorded two albums in this series—*Michigan* (2003), a downbeat, folky evocation of Stevens' home state, and 2005's *Come On Feel the Illinoise*, a tour de force of baroque folk-pop, full of beautiful arrangements, flutes, strings, brass, banjo, and vibes. Next came *The Age of Adz* (2010), a brilliantly weird record of apocalyptic, sci-fi angst focused on mortality and sexual jealousy. The tone and title were inspired by the outsider artist Royal Roberts, but also by a viral infection that Stevens suffered in the run-up to writing the album. He reacted against the folk sound of previous work by constructing bold, electronic compositions with weird, atonal sound effects and long passages of distorted vocals reminiscent of Kanye's *808s*

& Heartbreak (see page 130). There's not a banjo in earshot, but just to be contrary he simultaneously released *All Delighted People* (2010), an hour-long EP of acoustic songs.

Sufjan returned to acoustic domesticity for *Carrie & Lowell* (2015) named after his mother, who had died in 2012, and stepfather. He wrote the songs as a way of mourning his mother, who had suffered from mental illness and addiction. It's a beautiful and at times harrowing meditation on loss and abandonment.

Stevens has since released an Oscar-nominated song for 2017 film *Call Me By Your Name*, singles in celebration of Pride and about Tonya Harding, a collaborative album inspired by the planets of the solar system and another based on a ballet. Phew! His latest album is *Aporia* (2020), an almost instrumental synth record, co-created with his stepfather Lowell Brams.

TOP ALBUM *Come On Feel the Illinoise* (2005) This covers a stunning range of moods and musical styles, from the epic sweep of "Chicago" to the quiet sadness of "Casimir Pulaski Day." Lyrically he covers everything from UFO sightings to serial killer John Wayne Gacy Jr. He had so much material left over that he made a 21-track album of offcuts, *The Avalanche* (2006), which is almost as good.

POP TRIVIA Stevens has made two festive collections, *Songs for Christmas* (2006) and *Silver & Gold* (2012). He has spoken of his ambiguous relationship with the holidays, which explains titles like "Did I Make You Cry On Christmas Day? (Well, You Deserved It!)."

The Flaming Lips

By the time the new century rolled around, The Flaming Lips had actually been toiling at the psychedelic coalface for almost 20 years, but their breakthrough to a wider audience came with *The Soft Bulletin* in 1999 and *Yoshimi Battles The Pink Robots* in 2002.

The band formed in Oklahoma, Planet Earth, in 1983, originally with Wayne Coyne's brother Mark on lead vocals. Their early material had the flavor of punk and hard rock, sounding more like The Jesus and Mary Chain (see page 53) than The Flaming Lips, as they would come to be known and loved. Over the course of the 1980s and '90s, they gradually became more experimental, augmenting their sound with tape loops and studio effects, and developing their neo-psychedelic take on rock music. Things got noticeably weirder on the brilliantly titled *In A Priest Driven Ambulance* (1990) and they had a surprise hit with the goofy "She Don't Use Jelly" from 1993's *Transmissions From The Satellite Heart*. In 1997 they indulged their experimental excesses by releasing *Zaireeka*, an album consisting of four CDs that were designed to be played simultaneously.

On their breakthrough record, *The Soft Bulletin* (1999), they reined in their wildest impulses, marrying sonic weirdness to lushly orchestrated songs with a lighter, poppier feel than their earlier work. The album brought to the fore Wayne Coyne's penchant for B-movie scenarios, as on the popular single "Race for the Prize," which imagines two scientists striving to save humanity from an unnamed medical catastrophe. Also present was Coyne's love of half-baked metaphysical speculation and zany sense of humor. One track's full title is "What Is the Light? (An Untested Hypothesis Suggesting That the Chemical [In Our Brains] by Which We Are Able to Experience the Sensation of Being in Love Is the Same Chemical That Caused the 'Big Bang' That Was the Birth of the Accelerating Universe)." On "The Spiderbite Song" he reflected on the respective near-death experiences of band-mates Steven Drodz and Michael Ivins.

On 2002's *Yoshimi Battles The Pink Robots*, the band further honed their brand of catchy, metaphorical space-pop. The title track is in the same vein as "Race for the Prize," and imagines Yoshimi as a Japanese super-girl battling Godzilla-esque monsters on our behalf. The band added another enduring classic to their repertoire with "Do You Realize," a moving ode to the transience of life. Their next album, *At War with the Mystics* (2006), continued the trick of balancing affecting songwriting and sonic experimentation, but added a healthy dose of fuzzy funk and glam rock to their sound.

In truth, Wayne Coyne is not the best singer in the world (or cosmos), but he is a charismatic frontman and a great hatcher of harebrained schemes, leading his band into strange new vistas. He wrote and directed *Christmas On Mars* (2008), a science fiction movie starring the band, which was about Mars colonists celebrating Yuletide. In addition to recording two more studio albums, *Embryonic* (2009) and the bleak *The Terror* (2013), the band have collaborated with other musicians, including Nick Cave (see page 96) and Bon Iver's Justin Vernon (see page 146), Henry Rollins and Peaches, both on their *Heady Fwends* record (2012) and on a series of bizarre covers albums that reinterpret classic records by Pink Floyd, King Crimson, The Stone Roses (see page 92), and The Beatles. In recent years, Coyne has struck up a surprising friendship with Miley Cyrus. She contributed to their Sgt. Pepper record *With A Little Help From My Fwends* (2014) and in turn the band co-wrote and co-produced her album *Miley Cyrus & Her Dead Petz* (2015). The Flaming Lips' 2019 concept album *King's Mouth* is narrated by The Clash's Mick Jones (see page 21). The Flaming Lips also contributed a song called "SpongeBob & Patrick Confront the Psychic Wall of Energy" to *The SpongeBob SquarePants Movie*. Seriously, check it out—it's one of my favorite things they've done!

TOP ALBUM *With A Little Help From My Fwends* (2014) Perhaps this bizarre, pitch-shifting, squelchy re-imagining of *Sgt. Pepper's Lonely Hearts Club Band* (1967) is the closest I'll get to experiencing the impact of The Beatles' LSD-tinged revelation in 1967. I'm not going to claim that I'd take this over the original record, but it's a thrillingly bonkers listen all the same. Rolling out the Auto-tune for "With A Little Help From My Friends" is a stroke of genius.

POP TRIVIA The Flaming Lips are renowned for their elaborate live performances, which feature dazzling pyrotechnics, light shows, and video projections, and frequently dancers in animal costumes. Not content with normal crowdsurfing, Wayne Coyne has taken to "zorbing" out into the crowd in his own plastic bubble.

QUEENS OF THE STONE AGE

In addition to being the best-looking man in rock, Josh Homme possesses a fine croon. Since 1996, he has been pairing this with pounding guitars to great effect with his band Queens of the Stone Age.

QOTSA are known for a sassy take on desert rock, characterized by repetitive monster riffs and Homme's laid-back singing style. They grew out of the demise of his previous band Kyuss and released their eponymous debut in 1998. Fellow Kyuss veteran Nick Oliveri joined the band soon after and appeared on their second album, *Rated R* (2000). This spawned one of the band's most popular songs, "The Lost Art Of Keeping A Secret," which boats a particularly fine Homme croon. Oliveri was the other mainstay of the band's early line-up, which otherwise used a revolving cast of alt-rock musicians, including The Screaming Trees' Mark Lanegan and some guy called Dave Grohl. Oliveri had a reputation as the biggest hell-raiser in a band of hell-raisers and a tendency to, erm, let it all hang out when playing live. He was eventually fired by Homme in 2004.

QOTSA's breakthrough album was 2002's *Songs For The Deaf*, featuring what would become their signature song, "No One Knows" (another good Homme crooner). In addition to Homme and Oliveri, *Songs For The Deaf* featured Grohl on drums and contributions from Lanegan, Alain Johannes, Natasha Shneider, and Gene Trautmann. It remains their most popular album.

Homme and co. followed up with the stylistically varied *Lullabies To Paralyze* in 2005 and the industrial-sounding *Era Vulgaris* in 2007. Fans had to wait until 2013 for the band's sixth album—*Like Clockwork*, which features previous QOTSA musicians, including Grohl and Olivier, as well as the Arctic Monkeys' Alex Turner (see page 120), the Scissor Sisters' Jake Shears, and, erm, Elton John! By contrast, 2017's *Villains* stripped things back to the core band, but enlisted super-producer Mark Ronson to help create its spiky funk-rock corners.

TOP ALBUM *Songs For The Deaf* (2002) The album's concept is a road journey, featuring interjections from bizarre DJs. This gives the band an excuse to play with different styles and tempos, as if you're surfing the radio waves. "No One Knows" is weirder than you remember, equal parts Lou Reed oompah music and glam stomp. But there's also the honky-tonk gonzo rock of "Go With The Flow" and the astonishing final track "Mosquito Song," which suddenly pulls a chamber orchestra out of its pocket.

POP TRIVIA Josh Homme's a busy guy. In addition to QOTSA, he formed supergroup Them Crooked Vultures with Dave Grohl and Led Zep bassist John Paul Jones and co-founded Eagles of Death Metal. He has hosted the legendary Desert Sessions in Joshua Tree, California, and has produced artists, including the Arctic Monkeys and Iggy Pop (see page 18). He also found time to cameo in the cult comedy *Toast of London*.

TV ON THE RADIO

Like Animal Collective (see page 133), TV On The Radio have an "anything goes" attitude and, like Radiohead (see page 94), they mix rock instrumentation and electronic programming to create music that oscillates between synthetic and organic sounds.

TV On The Radio songs incorporate drones, jazz skronks, and Krautrock riffs. Melody seems to coalesce gradually out of the noise, carried by Tunde Adebimpe's soulful vocals (he frequently sings a mean falsetto). Adebimpe and guitarist/producer Dave Sitek recorded a demo CD *OK Calculator* (a nod to Radiohead) in 2002 and then recruited multi-instrumentalist Kyp Malone for the EP *Young Liars*, which included a spooky cappella cover of the Pixies' song "Mr Grieves." (Kyp Malone rocks a fine beard and afro, which make him look strangely like a black Karl Marx. Can we persuade him to release an album under that name?)

Their first album proper was *Desperate Youth, Bloodthirsty Babes* (2004), which established them as forward-thinking rock experimentalists. One fan with some form in experimental pop music was David Bowie who dropped by during the recording of their second album, *Return to Cookie Mountain* (2006), to add some backing vocals to the song "Province." The album also includes "Wolf Like Me," which remains their biggest-selling single in the US.

Dear Science (2008) leavened the angsty atmosphere with funk and dance rhythms, noticeably on "Crying," "Red Dress," and the infectious "Dancing Choose." Tragically, the band's bass player, Gerard Smith, died of lung cancer the week after they released their fourth album, *Nine Types of Light* (2011). TV On The Radio have thus far released one more album, 2014's *Seeds*. Though typically eclectic, *Seeds* emphasizes the dancey side of the band.

TOP ALBUM *Desperate Youth, Bloodthirsty Babes* (2004) is the aural equivalent of chucking everything at the wall to see what sticks. The album opens with a burst of jazz saxophone and then a piledriver of treated guitar, before Adebimpe's vocals improbably stitch it all together. From then on, it's anyone's guess what's coming next. "Staring At The Sun" and "Dreams" both combine sweet soul harmonies with doomy electro drones and "Ambulance" invents "Alt-barbershop."

POP TRIVIA In addition to producing his own band, Dave Sitek has produced music for many other artists, including (deep breath) Yeah Yeah Yeahs, Foals, Little Dragon, Beady Eye (see page 86), Kelis, Scarlett Johansson, and Beyoncé and Jay-Z.

The Strokes

Is This It? We certainly thought so in 2001 when The Strokes released their debut album, dripping with lo-fi New York cool.

After the earnest angst of grunge and copycat predictability of Britpop, The Strokes were a breath of fresh air. Their choppy, distorted guitars, short songs, and Julian Casablancas' Lou-Reed-esque drawl alluded to the glory years of New York rock, and *Is This It* sounded like it had been recorded in a tenement basement between cigarette breaks. The band looked the part: five elegantly wasted young men with lank hair and thrift-store clothes. Sales of secondhand blazer jackets shot up overnight.

The members of the band met while studying at various posh schools in New York, France, and Switzerland. Slumming it back in New York, they recorded *The Modern Age* EP—released in the UK before the US by Rough Trade Records—which sparked a bidding war to sign the band. RCA won the battle but delayed the release of the debut album because of concerns over its iconic yet ludicrous artwork (a photo of a gloved hand on a naked woman's behind, surely a nod to Spinal Tap) and the song "New York City Cops," which was considered insensitive in the aftermath of the 9/11 attacks. *Is This It* was eventually released in the US without the offending song and with dreadful replacement artwork. Crap artwork would become a feature of future Strokes' releases.

Their follow-up record, *Room On Fire* (2003), continued The Strokes' sound of lo-fi metronomic guitars and Casablancas' switching between laconic drawl and throat-shredding roar, but added other flavors to the pot, including hints of ska ("Automatic Shop") and romantic balladry in the vein of Jonathan Richman ("Under Control"). 2006's *First Impressions Of Earth* was received less favorably but still contained great moments, not least the "Peter-Gunn"-quoting single "Juicebox." *Angles* (2011) had an absolutely horrible cover and the album itself wasn't great either. The recording process was apparently plagued with problems, not least a breakdown in communication between Casablancas and the rest of the band. The Strokes' thrift-store chic had become tiresome and the band was understandably looking for new musical direction, but *Angles* mainly sounds confused, at times harking back to *Is This It,* at others invoking '80s rock or trying to be MGMT. *Comedown Machine* (2013) also mixes musical styles to varying degrees of success. "One Way Trigger" sounds like the band have stumbled into a klezmer party, while "80's Comedown Machine" is a more pleasing stylistic departure. In 2020, the band released *The New Abnormal,* produced by Rick Rubin and wrapped in artwork by legendary New York painter Jean-Michel Basquiat. In truth, the band have never quite recaptured the impact of their debut, but perhaps that's asking too much of a group who stumbled upon a signature sound at exactly the right time, and whose unpolished early work was hyped to the hilt.

TOP ALBUM *Is This It* (2001) I could try and be cool and choose something less obvious, but it's got to be the debut, with or without the arse photo cover. It's hard to put your finger on just why it works so well. I suspect the young band had no idea what they were doing, but this lack of overthinking may be part of the trick. The stripped-back songs exude attitude and wasted bravado. "Some Day" and "Last Nite" have become indie disco classics and "New York City Cops," included on the non-US release, is also a rowdy, sing-along delight.

POP TRIVIA Julian Casablancas has released a solo album and two albums with his band The Voidz. Guitarist Albert Hammond Jr. has released four solo albums, as well as his own line of suits. So, you too can now get The Strokes' look!

THE WHITE STRIPES

Jack and Meg White's lo-fi garage blues captured the imagination of music fans in the early 2000s.

The White Stripes were an exercise in doing a lot with not much—just two musicians with a cranked-up electric guitar and a stripped-down drum kit. Despite, or perhaps because of, this setup, their gigs were legendarily incendiary affairs, with Jack White manically riffing over Meg's simplistic drumming. They recorded albums quickly, in a matter of weeks, on analog equipment and dressed themselves and their records in a uniform of red, white, and black. The duo mischievously claimed to be brother and sister. In fact, they had been married, but were separated by the time the band came to prominence. Confused?

By 2000 they already had two albums under their belts, but it was 2001's *White Blood Cells* that broke them to a wider audience. The album's two lead singles summarized the breadth of their sound. "Hotel Yorba" was an acoustic skiffle yarn propelled by Meg's child-like drumming, while "Fell in Love with a Girl" was a manic, garage-rock vamp, like Buzzcocks (see page 24) transported to Louisiana. Over its 16 short songs, Jack White wrestled a surprising number of moods and effects out of the band's basic guitar and drums setup.

2003's *Elephant* was recorded at London's Toe Rag studios on vintage recording equipment. (The liner notes boasted that no equipment from after 1963 was used.) Though sticking largely to the same formula, Jack White added dashes of piano to fill out the sound and created multi-tracked harmonies with his vocals. He largely put the electric guitar aside for the next album, *Get Behind Me Satan* (2005), instead concentrating on acoustic guitar, piano, and occasional marimba and mandolin. Having said that, the album opens with "Blue Orchid," which is built around one of his most monstrous riffs.

For their final album, entitled *Icky Thump* (2007), they returned to a heavier blues-rock sound, although taking scenic detours into mariachi and Scottish folk music. Despite being recorded entirely in Nashville, the record displayed their Anglophile tendencies. The title is adapted from the Lancashire expression "ecky thump" and, confusingly, on the cover Jack and Meg are dressed in the Pearly King and Queen costumes of east London.

The White Stripes petered out rather than falling apart. The band's last tour was in support of *Icky Thump* in 2007 and Jack White finally announced that the band was no more in 2011. By this time he was busy with various musical projects. He has toured and recorded with his bands The Raconteurs and The Dead Weather, as well as releasing three solo albums. He's also produced music for other artists, including Loretta Lynn and the Smoke Fairies. Perhaps most significantly he founded Third Man Records, an independent record company and studio in Nashville that's dedicated to recording and releasing music on vinyl.

TOP ALBUM *Elephant* (2003) This contains many of the band's best moments, including the irresistible "Seven Nation Army," and the bruising "The Hardest Button To Button." On "There's No Home For You Here," White stacks his vocals to make a choir of backing Jacks and wrings extraordinary noises from his guitar.

POP TRIVIA The White Stripes made occasional forays into film. Jack White acted in and recorded music for the Anthony Minghella movie *Cold Mountain* (2003). Jack and Meg appeared as themselves in Jim Jarmusch's *Coffee and Cigarettes* (2003), waxing lyrical about the achievements of pioneering inventor Nikola Tesla.

WHY THE WHITE STRIPES SPLIT UP...

MEG! DID YOU WASH THE REDS AND WHITES TOGETHER!?

ARCADE FIRE

Arcade Fire are the sound of artsy, literate angst in the 21st century. Not for nothing were they endorsed by the original art-rocker David Bowie (who sang backing vocals on "Reflektor").

Like Bowie (see page 10), the band have a taste for the dramatic, with Win Butler's semi-histrionic vocals at the forefront of unusual arrangements that incorporate strings, accordion, and pounding drums. The band has a skewed take on pop music, even if it's sometimes hard to put your finger on what it is that sounds odd. There's often a David-Lynch-esque sense of disquiet, of something menacing lurking just beneath the surface.

Arcade Fire are from Montreal, Canada, although Win Butler and his brother Will Butler (who's also in the band) were brought up as Mormons in the US. Win Butler's wife, Régine Chassagne, is also in the band. The Butlers clearly subscribe to the theory that the family that plays together stays together. Chassagne is of Haitian descent, her parents having fled to Canada from the dictatorship of François Duvalier. In "Haiti," on the band's debut album *Funeral* (2004), she sings, in French and English, about the deaths of Haitians at Duvalier's hands. *Funeral* was a big success for the band. Audiences responded to its moody songs of ambiguous desperation and euphoria, in particular "Rebellion (Lies)" and the epic "Wake Up."

The follow-up album, 2007's *Neon Bible*, upped the ante on their debut, exploring the band's full dynamic range, from fragile beauty to euphoric release. Highlights include the sinister disquiet of "Black Mirror," the over-the-top, church-organ pomp of "Intervention," and the epic sing-along "No Cars Go." *The Suburbs* (2010) stretched their songwriting ambitions even further, across a double album of 16 songs inspired by the Butler boys' upbringing in The Woodlands, a suburb of Houston, Texas.

The band took a dancier direction for *Reflektor* (2013), drafting in LCD Soundsystem's James Murphy (see page 122) to produce, along with sessions with their regular producer Markus Dravs. This is another double album, influenced by Butler and Chassagne's increasing interest in Haitian culture, and its Rara music in particular. Butler's lyrics were also influenced by "The Present Age," an 1846 essay by Søren Kierkegaard, don't you know. Arcade Fire released their fifth album in 2017. Like its predecessor, *Everything Now* is an uptempo dancey affair, but haunted by the band's trademark sense of unease.

TOP ALBUM *The Suburbs* (2010) Win Butler has said that he wanted *The Suburbs* to sound like the music of his youth, a mixture of Depeche Mode and Neil Young. Its songs have a strange tendency to creep up on you, sounding at first conventional and then revealing their weirdness. This is especially true of the title track and the incredible "We Used To Wait," which starts out like a honky-tonk lament and then goes... somewhere else.

POP TRIVIA The debut album was named *Funeral* because several band members lost relatives during the recording process. Chief among these was the Butlers' maternal grandfather Alvino Rey. Rey was a swing band musician, radio operator, and inventor, who continued to play music into his 90s. He was a pioneer of the pedal steel guitar and quite possibly the first to electronically amplify a stringed instrument.

CHOOSING A BAND NAME...

wilco

Chicago's Wilco have been described as the "country Radiohead," and it's a decent comparison as far as it goes.

Under the leadership of craggy-faced frontman Jeff Tweedy, they create beautiful, anthemic country rock with an experimental twist. A Wilco song might start out as a gentle country ballad, or even a bit of good time honky-tonk, before phasing into atonal guitars and electronic walls of static.

Wilco actually formed in the mid-1990s, but it was their fourth album *Yankee Hotel Foxtrot*, released in 2001, that established their reputation as a pioneering, experimental band. Tweedy brought in Jim O'Rourke to mix the record and from the opening bars of "I Am Trying To Break Your Heart," you knew you were in strange terrain. The album's songs were peppered with atmospheric distortion and mechanical drones, country melodies rubbing up against industrial squalls. They wisely turned the weirdness off for country-soul gem "Jesus, Etc." which sits like an untarnished pearl in the middle of the album. The atmosphere also cheers up briefly for the goofy "Heavy Metal Drummer." The making of *Yankee Hotel Foxtrot* was a fraught affair of musical differences and personnel changes. The documentary *I Am Trying To Break Your Heart: A Film About Wilco* captured this period, which culminated in second songwriter Jay Bennett leaving the band.

Wilco worked with O'Rourke on their next album, *A Ghost Is Born* (2004). If anything it was even odder than *Yankee Hotel Foxtrot*. They have released four studio albums since, running the gamut from acoustic folk to extreme noise, often on the same record. 2015's cheekily named *Star Wars* was given away as a free download from their website for a limited period. *Schmilco* (2016) was a largely chilled out affair and featured album artwork by cult illustrator Joan Cornellà. The band's 11th album, *Ode to Joy* (2019) is stark and spacious but with uplifting moments befitting of its

title. Wilco have also released three volumes of *Mermaid Avenue,* a collaborative project with socialist troubadour Billy Bragg to write new music for the orphaned lyrics of Woody Guthrie. Jeff Tweedy has recorded three solo albums, an album with his son Spencer, and has worked with musicians including White Denim (see page 140) and soul legend Mavis Staples.

TOP ALBUM *A Ghost Is Born* (2004) Wilco haven't made a bad album but this is the one I go back to most often. It's an obstinate, cantankerous beast. It does its best to scare off the casual listener by opening with its two most maudlin songs, followed by a ten-minute Krautrock wig-out. It then rewards you with three of the band's loveliest songs, "Muzzle of Bees," "Hummingbird," and "Handshake Drugs," before plunging back into atonal fuzz and gloom. It's an emotional rollercoaster alright.

POP TRIVIA In 2001, *Yankee Hotel Foxtrot* was rejected by Wilco's then-record label Reprise and the band were dropped from the label. Reprise were a subsidiary of Warner, which was cutting costs at the time. Reprise allowed them to take the tapes with them, reportedly for free, and after streaming the album on their own website, Wilco sold it to Nonesuch Records, *also* a subsidiary of Warner. The music biz, eh? *Yankee Hotel Foxtrot* went on to be Wilco's biggest-selling record.

Franz Ferdinand

Franz Ferdinand, Archduke of Austria-Hungary, was shot on June 28, 1914, pitching Europe into the First World War. Oh, no hang on... sorry.

Franz Ferdinand was formed by Alex Kapranos, Nick McCarthy, Bob Hardy, and Paul Thomson in Glasgow in 2002. There's clearly something in the waters of the Clyde—see also Belle and Sebastian (page 104), Primal Scream (page 93), and my wife. FF's music combines an art-school sensibility with a sassy, dance-friendly take on punk-pop. The band said they wanted to make music that girls could dance to and they were heavily influenced by '70s CBGB's bands, such as Blondie (see page 9). Their early artwork and videos referenced Russian artists such as Rodchenko, as well as European Dada and Surrealism. In general, the band embodied an image that was arty and literate yet also, erm, sexy.

Their 2004 debut, *Franz Ferdinand* (2004), was a hit on both sides of the Atlantic, propelled by the storming "Take Me Out." Though not explicitly about the historical Franz Ferdinand, its video contained numerous gun and target motifs, while the single's B-side "All For You" contained references to Franz Ferdinand's wife and their assassin. The album is great—full of wit, sparkle, and sassiness—and deservedly won the 2004 Mercury Music Prize. Their next album, *You Could Have It So Much Better* (2005), continued in this vein, developing Kapranos' lyrical talent for deadpan comedy, but also broadening their stylistic range, including the pretty chamber-pop of "Eleanor Put Your Boots On."

2009's *Tonight* was an ambitious but not totally successful foray into dub and dancier styles, packaged as a hedonistic concept album. 2013's *Right Thoughts, Right Words, Right Action* is more immediate than its predecessor. Overall it leans toward the disco-punk sound of their early work, but still demonstrates the influence of garage rock, dub, and dance from beyond the indie ghetto. The band produced the album themselves, but also recruited Hot Chip's Alexis Taylor and Joe Goddard (see page 123) and Norwegian producer Todd Terje to co-produce some tracks.

In 2015, FF teamed up with legendary avant-glam weirdos Sparks to form the eccentric supergroup, FFS. Nick McCarthy left the band in 2016 and Franz Ferdinand recorded *Always Ascending* (2018) with a new line-up.

TOP ALBUM *FFS* (2015) I'm going to cheat and choose this collaborative album with Sparks because it's the my favorite thing FF have done. It sounds exactly like a collaboration between the FF and S components, with the sounds of both bands intact, yet so much better than we had any reason to expect. The two groups seem to urge each other on to greater excesses. On songs like "Johnny Delusional," Kapranos and Ron Mael compete to see who can be the most arch vocalist, while "Police Encounters" is genuinely, thrillingly unhinged.

POP TRIVIA Before the band took off, Kapranos worked for a spell as a chef. Later he wrote a fortnightly column for the *Guardian* newspaper about his gastronomic adventures on tour. These pieces were later adapted into a book, *Sound Bites: Eating on Tour with Franz Ferdinand.*

ARCTIC MONKEYS

The first the great British public knew of the Arctic Monkeys was their debut single, the mighty "I Bet You Look Good on the Dancefloor," which went straight to Number One in October 2005.

This seemingly instant success was the result of some serious graft. Arctic Monkeys were one of the first bands to use the Internet effectively as a marketing tool, winning over large numbers of tech-literate young fans, not so much by word of mouth as word of myspace. Crucially, they backed up this online hype with blistering live gigs, establishing a reputation as one of the best unsigned bands on the circuit. By the time they did sign, with indie stalwarts Domino Records, and released that single, there was a huge buzz about the band.

While their approach was cutting edge, their sound harked back to punk and classic rock, filtered through the Britpop of 10 years previously when the band were kids, as well as older styles such as skiffle and even George Formby. Lyrically, Alex Turner's wordy and witty songs were reminiscent of fellow Sheffielder Jarvis Cocker (see page 81) and were influenced by the work of punk poet John Cooper Clarke, as well as hip-hop. The first two albums, *Whatever People Say I Am, That's What I'm Not* (2006) and *Favourite Worst Nightmare* (2007), are masterpieces in pithy urban observation, with Turner casting a weary eye over his hometown and skewering the behavior of inebriated youth on a Friday night. The songs are full of nightclub queues and bouncers, taxi ranks, and petty criminals. Was there ever a more English name for a song than "Mardy Bum"?

Still, this innate sense of Englishness didn't stop the band from going on to success in the US and elsewhere. For their third album, *Humbug* (2009), they recruited Josh Homme of Queens of the Stone Age (see page 110) to help them spread their wings in the Mojave Desert. Homme shared production duties with Simian Mobile Disco's James Ford, who had co-produced *Favourite Worst Nightmare* and would go on to record their subsequent albums *Suck It and See* (2011) and *AM* (2013). As the band's focus and experience became more international, so their sound changed, abandoning the hectic skiffle of their early work in favor of bigger grooves and stoner riffs.

AM (2013) made good on longstanding hints of the band's love of R&B, matching Turner's sultry croon with a chorus of falsetto backing vocals and some seriously slinky basslines. If that seemed a world away from Sheffield on a Friday night,

then their next album saw them break further out of their previous orbit. *Tranquility Base Hotel & Casino* (2018) imagines Turner and co as louche, time-worn residents of a luxury resort on the moon. The band's stylistic turn towards John Barry lounge pop and Serge Gainsbourg chanson (recalling Turner's side project The Last Shadow Puppets) polarised fans but I think it's great – an exotic, expansive new setting for Turner's droll lyrical observations.

TOP ALBUM *Favourite Worst Nightmare* (2007) This album continues in the vein of their debut, delivering a set of character assassinations and withering put-downs in a distinctly British vernacular. But it has more balls than the first album, as well as more variety in its sound. "Fluorescent Adolescent" sarcastically yet tenderly portrays a stale relationship and includes perhaps the only reference to a Mecca Bingo "dauber" pen in pop. Album-closer "505" hints at the more expansive sound the band would later develop and also at the sexier side of Alex Turner (he can use that as the title for his solo album).

POP TRIVIA Arctic Monkeys' musical development is paralleled by changes in their image. After falling in with indie troubadour and professional '50s throwback Richard Hawley, the band went from scruffy, second-generation Britpop scallies to elegant, rockabilly lotharios. Alex Turner, in particular, grew a quiff of such proportions that one feared for his slender frame. These days you would struggle to find a sharper dressed bunch of lads.

lcd soundsystem

Professionally disheveled musician and producer James Murphy knows his way around a dirty electronic groove and a memorable, laconic lyric.

Murphy started releasing material as LCD Soundsystem on DFA Records, which he had co-founded. His first single, the self-mocking hipster's lament "Losing My Edge," became an underground hit in 2002. In 2005, LCD Soundsystem released its eponymous album. The record came with two discs, one containing the album and the other "Losing My Edge" and other subsequent singles. The album proper was received well, not least because of its brilliant lead-off single "Daft Punk Is Playing At My House," in which Murphy claims, somewhat unconvincingly, that he has secured the services of the French robots for his house party. Though presented primarily as a dance record, the album also shows off Murphy's rockier influences. "On Repeat" nods toward The Fall (see page 48) and "Never As Tired As When I'm Waking Up" has a flavor of *White-Album*-era Beatles.

Murphy played the vast majority of the instruments himself on the debut, but he recruited musicians from other acts on his label, including Hot Chip guitarist Al Doyle (see page 123), to play live and to contribute to later recordings. LCD Soundsystem released two more studio albums, *Sound of Silver* (2007) and *This Is Happening* (2010). If Murphy never quite managed another track as effortlessly cool as "Daft Punk...," these albums are still stuffed to the gills with slinky beats and grooves. *This Is Happening* includes the rowdy ode to bacchanalia, "Drunk Girls."

In 2011, Murphy announced the end of LCD Soundsystem and in April of that year he played an epic, four-hour farewell show at Madison Square Garden, with guest performers including Arcade Fire (see page 116). A live album of this concert was later released as *The Long Goodbye* (2014). However, Murphy released an anti-Christmas single "Christmas Will Break Your Heart" in December 2015 and in 2017 LCD Soundsystem released their fourth album *American Dream*. It includes squelchy earworm "Tonite" and "Black Screen", a mournful 12-minute tribute to David Bowie.

TOP ALBUM *Sound of Silver* (2007) This is a pleasing collision of all of Murphy's pop and artsy influences. On "North American Scum," he repeats his trick of ranting sarcastically over a catchy groove. "Someone Great" and "Sound of Silver" nod to The Human League, while "All My Friends" sounds like minimalist composer Steve Reich covering the Arcade Fire. The album closes with "New York, I Love You But You're Bringing Me Down," a slow-building torch song of urban alienation, like the disenchanted reflection of Sinatra's "New York, New York."

POP TRIVIA LCD Soundsystem's sound has had an influence beyond its popularity with a fervent few. Murphy became an in-demand producer, and the man you went to if you wanted to inject your guitar band with an adrenalin shot of credible dance music. He has worked as producer and re-mixer with acts that include Arcade Fire, David Bowie (see page 10), Franz Ferdinand (see page 119), and Pulp (see page 81).

HOT CHIP

I love Hot Chip, and it's 90 per cent for the music, it really is, but I also love that they look so unlike dance musicians. The lead singer, Alexis Taylor, looks like Brains from *Thunderbirds*, if *Thunderbirds* was set in a bank; Joe Goddard resembles a pub landlord; Felix Martin looks like he should be lecturing in semiotics; and is that Vincent Van Gogh on guitar?!

This isn't just me being mean for comic effect; it's a clue to what makes Hot Chip special. Their music is dance music made by nerds, R&B reprocessed by white, middle-class geeks. The band know how to play this disconnect for laughs when they choose, as on their debut album, *Coming On Strong* (2004), on which Taylor makes some surprisingly lewd suggestions and boasts of the band's musical prowess in an unconvincing hip-hop style.

Hot Chip's sonically adventurous second album, *The Warning* (2005), brought them to greater attention, in particular their propulsively catchy single "Over and Over" and it's folk-tronic follow-up "Boy from School." The band have released five albums since. 2008's *Made In The Dark* had a more boisterous feel, which was partially the result of including more live performance in the recording process. Along the way, Taylor has evolved a fine way with an understated love song, as evidenced by the charming title track of 2010's *One Life Stand*. 2015's *Why Make Sense?* features moody single "Huarache Lights," named after a pair of Nike trainers, and the romantic ballad "White Wine and Fried Chicken."

Performing live, the band used to play in a straight line across the stage, like a scruffier Kraftwerk (see page 38), but abandoned this arrangement with the addition of drumming virtuoso Sarah Jones. Their latest album has the tongue-in-cheek, provocative title *A Bathful of Ecstasy* (2019) and incorporates material originally written by Taylor and Goddard for pop princess Katy Perry.

TOP ALBUM *In Our Heads* (2012) This contains many of my favorite Hot Chip moments, including "How Do You Do?", synth-pop/funk mash-up "Don't Deny Your Heart," and, best of all, the absolute banger "Night & Day."

POP TRIVIA The members of Hot Chip have kept busy with DJ slots and other extra-curricular projects. Alexis Taylor has released solo albums and collaborated with various musicians, including David Byrne (see page 34) in the Atomic Bomb! Band, performing the music of Nigerian funk musician William Onyeabor. Joe Goddard formed the dance act 2 Bears with Raf Rundell, while guitarist Al Doyle (aka Van Gogh) has played with LCD Soundsystem (see page 122).

AMY WINEHOUSE

In the mid- to late 2000s, Amy Winehouse was a chart-topping, critically lauded, larger-than-life PROPER POP STAR, before it all descended into horrible tabloid tragedy.

It shouldn't have worked. Winehouse's music was so rooted in the musical tropes of earlier decades that it should have come off as retro kitsch. The spot-on recreations of '50s and '60s jazz and soul by her producers, Salaam Remi and Mark Ronson, should have sounded like pale imitations. Yet somehow it worked beautifully. It was partially THAT VOICE: full of conviction and brimming with natural talent in an age of anaemic TV talent show performances. In 2003, it was a novelty to hear a singer so blatantly alluding to the soulful, jazzy stylings of earlier music previously roped off in a historical ghetto. Yet somehow her records also sounded contemporary and managed to bring those classic musical styles back into the mainstream. It's impossible to imagine chart-topping pop diva Adele without Winehouse paving her way.

From the start of debut album, *Frank* (2003), Winehouse established her public image as self-destructive party girl, sexually voracious and yet fatally attracted to the wrong man. In this she drew on the image and life histories of earlier jazz singers, notably Billie Holiday, but it also proved to be tragically prescient. Life imitating art or art imitating life? Winehouse and Remi created a jazzy vibe, a contemporary take on smoky nightclub ballads, but also with nods to hip-hop sampling.

On the follow-up, *Back To Black* (2006), Winehouse brought her template (slightly) more up to date, focusing on '60s girl groups, soul, and Motown. If *Frank* was a promising debut by a new artist, *Back To Black* became an honest-to-god pop phenomenon, catapulting Winehouse into the upper echelons of fame in the UK and then worldwide. The public responded to her songs' effortless pop hooks (snappily produced by Remi and transatlantic wunderkind Mark Ronson) and girls, in particular, empathized with the tales of hedonistic and romantic distress. She had created a soul soundtrack for the binge-drinking generation.

Winehouse's tragic wastrel image was only strengthened in the public imagination when her life appeared to slide out of control into a paparazzi-haunted nightmare of substance abuse, failed marriage, and the ultimate ignominy of being photographed with Pete Doherty. She appeared unable to sing at gigs due to intoxication, and concerts, then whole tours, were canceled. A third album was promised, but never appeared. Contrary to the claims of her biggest hit, she did go to rehab and her recoveries and relapses became the subject of endless tabloid reports, as the UK gutter press found a favorite new person to harass. I'm sure this did record sales no harm, but it definitely harmed Amy Winehouse. The slow-mo tragedy of her decline ended with her death from alcohol poisoning on July 23, 2011 at the age of 27.

After her death, Winehouse's family established the Winehouse Foundation, a charity to help young people, which focuses on substance addiction. Her life and career were covered in the excellent, Oscar-winning documentary *Amy*, though the film drew criticism from her family.

TOP ALBUM *Back To Black* (2006) This is one of those albums so stuffed full of great pop songs that you can't believe they're all on the same record. It included most of her greatest moments, "Rehab," "You Know I'm No Good," "Back To Black," and "Tears Dry On Their Own," among them. The only thing missing is her cover of The Zutons' "Valerie," which is annoyingly on Mark Ronson's album *Special* (2007).

POP TRIVIA Her iconic beehive was apparently a weave created by her stylist. Winehouse's hairdo, makeup, and style were an effective combination of classic pop references, drawn from girl groups such as The Ronettes, as well as Bettie Page, mod, and rockabilly girls.

FLEET FOXES

Is there anything more reassuring than five hairy men in plaid harmonizing?

Fleet Foxes set out their stall early—stunningly beautiful, acoustic folk-pop with intricate vocal harmonies. The first song most of us heard by the band was the lead single from their debut album, *Fleet Foxes* (2008), the gorgeous "White Winter Hymnal." Lyrically, it's hard to tell what's going on in the song. There's a hint of violence, but the snowy setting created an image of the band as bucolic ruralists. This impression was only reinforced by pictures of the band. Singer Robin Pecknold and co. looked like they'd wandered straight out of *The Last Waltz* (Scorsese's concert film of The Band), got lost in a snowstorm, and emerged in 2008.

Indeed, Pecknold and lead guitarist Skyler Skjelset had bonded over their love of '60s and '70s rock and folk, including Bob Dylan, The Band, The Beach Boys, and Neil Young (see page 27). Disappointingly, they had done this in an affluent suburb of Seattle rather than on the porch of a cabin in the snowy wilderness. As with Amy Winehouse (see page 124), this harking back to an earlier sound should have left their music sounding slavishly imitative, but they did it with such skill and panache that it sounded fresh. Audiences in Europe, and to a lesser extent in the US, were bewitched by the emotional swell and lush harmonies of the debut album.

After touring extensively for three years, the band released their second album, *Helplessness Blues* (2011), a darker but equally rich offering of sumptuous melodies with characteristic harmonies. Highlights include the title track and "Battery Kinzie." After touring in support of *Helplessness Blues*, the band went on hiatus. There were hints of activity in the subsequent years and the silence was finally broken in 2017 with *Crack-Up*, the band's typically dense, sophisticated and lyrically abstruse third album. Though the music sounded hairier than ever Pecknold and his bandmates appeared disappointingly clean shaven and short haired in promotional photos and videos.

I saw Fleet Foxes in concert after the first album. I suspect it was a great gig if you were near the front but I made the mistake of staying near the back of the venue. Without much sight of the band it was curiously unsatisfying. They played *so well* and the harmonies were *so* spot-on, I could have been listening to the CD!

TOP ALBUM *Fleet Foxes* (2008) All three albums are great but the debut marginally wins out for me. Get lost in those soaring melodies, lush arrangements, and, yes, sorry to go on about them, beautiful harmonies. Get the deluxe version, which has bonus tracks including "Mykonos," to my mind their best song.

POP TRIVIA Drummer J. Tillman quit the band in 2012 and has since re-emerged as concept-folk-character (possibly) Father John Misty (see page 154).

elbow

Manchester's Elbow have cornered the market in lovelorn laments with uplifting anthemic choruses. It is now a legal requirement in the UK for all large sporting and cultural events to feature an Elbow song. Still, it's been a long journey from moody outsiders to the borders of national-treasure status.

Elbow formed in the early 1990s and, following a near miss in the late '90s when they were dropped from Island Records, released their debut album, *Asleep in the Back*, in 2001. Moody opening track "Any Day Now" is a personal favorite and the album established their signature sound of melancholic, careworn ballads. You can hear the influence of Radiohead (see page 94) and Jeff Buckley (see page 90), as well as Peter-Gabriel-era Genesis and Talk Talk. The next album, *Cast of Thousands* (2003), included weird gospel track "Ribcage," the exquisitely sad "Fugitive Motel," and the first of many Elbow sing-alongs, "Grace Under Pressure," for which the band recorded the crowd at Glastonbury singing the refrain "We still believe in love, so f*** you."

Elbow's fortunes continued to improve with 2005's *Leaders Of The Free World*, but the seal was put on their newfound popularity when their 2008 album *The Seldom Seen Kid* won the Mercury Music Prize. The Mercury also brought their music to a wider section of the British public, as did the use of *that* album's anthemic sing-along "One Day Like This" by the BBC for their coverage of the Beijing Olympics. The BBC also commissioned the band to write a theme for the 2012 London Olympics, which resulted in the ludicrously overblown "First Steps."

Elbow have released four more albums. *Little Fictions* (2017) includes songs recorded with Manchester's Hallé Orchestra and Choir. *Giants of All Sizes* (2019) has a terrible title but finds the band on robust form, its songs reckoning with the deaths of loved ones and British public traumas including Brexit and the Grenfell Fire. Singer Guy Garvey released his solo album *Courting The Squall* in 2015 and hosts a weekly radio show on BBC6 Music, on which he plays beautiful music, mainly by people he has bullied into being his friend.

TOP ALBUM *The Seldom Seen Kid* (2008) Not for nothing did this win them the Mercury. It's the band's most cohesive album, largely free of meandering and filled with well-crafted songs, including "The Bones of You," "Mirrorball," and the riff-tastic "Grounds for Divorce." Even on a cynical day, it's hard to resist the charms of the compulsory uplifting epic, "One Day Like This."

POP TRIVIA The band's name comes from Dennis Potter's brilliant TV drama *The Singing Detective*, whose protagonist explains that "elbow" is the most beautiful word in the English language. I love them just for that.

JOANNA NEWSOM

Joanna Newsom might be the antimatter reflection of a manufactured pop star, a virtuoso harpist blessed with an unusual singing voice who writes long, complex songs infused with surreal poetry and weaves strange musical tales involving fantastical characters.

Newsom grew up with a musical family in California but her baroque compositions owe something to the Appalachian folk music of the eastern US. Early press photos appeared to show an elf girl who had wandered south from some Tolkien-esque snowy land.

Her debut album, *The Milk-Eyed Mender* (2004), provoked "love it or hate it" responses. While many (myself included) thought we had an actual genius on our hands, others couldn't get beyond the weird intonations of her startling voice. The album's 12 songs ranged from wide-eyed wonder to tender sadness, via full-throated folk weirdness, all played by Newsom herself on the harp and piano with occasional harpsichord and Wurlitzer.

Her follow-up album, *Ys* (2006), was named after a mythical kingdom and was an altogether more ambitious affair. Inspired by his classic album *Song Cycle*, Newsom recruited legendary American musician and Beach Boys' collaborator Van Dyke Parks to produce and arrange her material for an accompanying orchestra. Newsom's vocals and harp were recorded by Steve Albini and the whole album was mixed by alt musican/producer (and sometime Sonic Youth member) Jim O'Rourke. Her then-boyfriend, alt-country musician Bill Callahan, also contributed backing vocals to one track. There are only five songs on *Ys*, ranging in length from 7 minutes ("Cosmia") to almost 17 ("Only Skin"). This gives the songs oodles of room to stretch and develop, Parks' arrangements shifting and shimmering beneath Newsom's plucked strings. Lyrically she uses the time to weave evocative poetic character descriptions or to tell strange tales, including one about a "Monkey & Bear."

Her next album, 2010's *Have One On Me*, was even more expansive, a triple album of songs whose only fault is that it takes two hours to listen to the whole thing and my brain isn't big enough to cope with it all. Suffice it to say that she broadens her palette yet further, adding jazzy and bluesy elements to her sound in songs that are occasionally reminiscent of that other great, adventurous songwriter Joni Mitchell (see page 12).

Newsom's fourth album, *Divers*, was released to great acclaim in 2015. She collaborated with a range of musicians for this one, including the City of Prague Philharmonic Orchestra.

TOP ALBUM *Divers* (2015) Newsom's latest album is more manageable a listen than its predecessor, but covers equal musical and emotional distance over its 11 tracks. Her lyrics frequently return to mortality and the fear of loss, while her harp and piano are woven through inventive arrangements involving myriad acoustic and electronic instruments. Her voice, meanwhile, has become an instrument of protean fluidity, at times hitting pure, choirboy high notes before swooping down into the eccentric toddler register of her early work.

POP TRIVIA Joanna Newsom is married to the comedy actor Andy Samberg. Yes, that's right, the guy from *Brooklyn Nine-Nine*. That's not her only link with the world of TV and film. She acted in and narrated Paul Thomas Anderson's movie *Inherent Vice* and he returned the favor by directing videos for her songs "Divers" and "Sapokanikan." Newsom also contributed a (very short) cameo to the theme tune for the 2011 *Muppets* movie. I think that's her at 0 minutes 27 seconds.

KANYE WEST

Kanye West confuses me. Life on Planet West/Kardashian appears to be an ongoing conveyor belt of excess, punctuated by semi-regular spats with other celebrities and unhinged pronouncements.

And yet, and yet... he's clearly very talented, a workaholic musician who has helped to steer hip-hop in a more interesting direction. It's pointless to try and divide Kanye the egomaniac celebrity from the musician, because celebrity excess is his biggest lyrical subject. But it's weird that for someone who is currently *so* famous, his songs aren't better known with the general public. That certainly wasn't the case with Michael Jackson. One thing that undoubtedly keeps his music off the radio is the frequency with which he drops the N-bomb (and yes, I realize that I sound like a grandad talking about pop music on the radio.)

Kanye on record is complicated, simultaneously decrying the shallowness of modern materialist culture, while boasting about his diamond-encrusted jewelry. Not for nothing did he sample the refrain from King Crimson's "21st Century Schizoid Man" on 2010's *My Beautiful Dark Twisted Fantasy*. Similarly, he's wont to play the wounded romantic, as on much of *808s & Heartbreak* (2008), but also indulges in nasty and graphic misogyny—listen to the horrible "Blame Game" on *My Beautiful Dark Twisted Fantasy* if you can bear it.

Kanye West albums are like huge brain-dumps, hundreds of contradictory ideas struggling to be heard. Is it possible that we're witnessing ADHD as art?! Of course, West cut his teeth as an in-house producer at Jay Z's Roc-A-Fella Records. At his best, he's an innovative producer, drawing on a wide variety of influences and samples, and bending them into strange new shapes. Check out his 2013 album *Yeezus* for the tribal, glam-rock beats of "Black Skinhead" and "Blood On The Leaves," which cuts up Nina Simone's version of "Strange Fruit" and then does amazing things with the pieces. *Yeezus* also includes "I Am A God," on which Kanye duets with, erm, God and demands that his croissants are brought to him with some haste. So, he's joking, right? Oh, I can't tell any more.

In February 2016 Kanye West released *The Life of Pablo*, through Jay Z and co's Tidal streaming service, but then continued to tinker with the recordings, updating them on Tidal as he went, explaining that the album was a "living, breathing, changing creative expression." Shortly after

releasing *The Life of Pablo*, he claimed to be millions of dollars in debt and took to Twitter to ask Mark Zuckerberg for a $1 billion investment in "Kanye West ideas." His next album, *Ye* (2018), packed an intense and exhaustive depiction of life on Planet West into its brief 28 minutes. The album cover featured the illuminating motto: "I hate being Bi-Polar its awesome". Earlier that year West had made controversial, culturally tone-deaf (to be charitable) statements about historical slavery in America, and in October 2018 he visited Trump in the Oval Office. In a beyond-parody, televised meeting he lavished praise on Trump while wearing a MAGA hat and, among other weirdnesses, pitched a hydrogen-powered plane to replace Air Force 1, inadvertently revealing his phone passcode to millions in the process.

His next album was announced only months after *Ye* with the typically modest name of *Yandhi* but in the event West postponed its release and reworked it as a typically hyperactive Christian, hip-hop, gospel record, *Jesus is King* (2019). It includes a sax solo from Kenny G. Thanks, Jesus.

TOP ALBUM *808s & Heartbreak* (2008) West responded to the untimely death of his mother and the breakup of a relationship by stripping everything back to synths, the 808 drum machine, and the dreaded Auto-tune. He largely eschews rapping in favor of soulful laments, crooned through the Auto-tune processor. It's a curious effect. At first it sounds ridiculous but, once you get used to it, it adds a mournful fluidity to his singing. The sound had a huge impact on other hip-hop and R&B acts, but also on alternative musicians such as Sufjan Stevens (see page 107).

POP TRIVIA Man, take your pick. His passcode is probably still 000000.

THE SCHOOL PRIZE FOR ACADEMIC ACHIEVEMENT GOES TO AMY JENKINS.

MY DAUGHTER, NORTH, WROTE ONE OF THE BEST ESSAYS OF ALL TIME!

AMY JENKINS NEEDS TO RESPECT REAL ACADEMIA!

DAAAAD!

Goldfrapp

Goldfrapp are two musicians, Alison Goldfrapp and Will Gregory, who have released seven albums, exploring an eclectic range of styles within the broad catch-all of electronic music.

Felt Mountain (2000), was lush and cinematic, with seductive vocals over soundscapes influenced by the film scores of Ennio Morricone and John Barry. The tone was beautiful but sinister, with hint of suppressed passion. 2003's *Black Cherry* was a more up-tempo, electro-pop take on glam rock. Alison Goldfrapp changed her image from Marlene-Dietrich-esque torch singer to aggressive new wave diva, often accompanied by wolves. Like Björk or Bowie (see pages 76 and 10), the band have self-consciously played with their image on each new release.

Supernature (2005) moved further into sexy disco, and the band had hits with "Ooh La La" and "Ride A White Horse." By contrast, 2008's *Seventh Tree* was gentle and pastoral, revisiting the haunting soundscapes of their debut but with the added warmth of acoustic guitars and strings. The accompanying imagery reflected the album's dreamlike atmosphere, with Alison wearing a Harlequin clown suit and bicorn hat. Goldfrapp swung back toward dance again for their next album, *Head First* (2010), which deliberately referenced cheesy synth-pop and mainstream rock such as Van Halen.

If Goldfrapp's music has always been cinematic, then they went the whole hog on *Tales of Us* (2013), a stark, melancholic suite of songs about 10 different characters. In 2014 they staged a screening of a film version of *Tales of Us*, directed by Lisa Gunning, which focuses on five of these characters. Their next album, *Silver Eye* (2017) seemed a deliberate synthesis of Goldfrapp's eclectic musical career thus far, incorporating the glam stomp of single "Anymore" and protean electronic soundscapes of "Faux Suede Drifter" and the beautiful "Moon in Your Mouth".

TOP ALBUM *Black Cherry* (2003) Goldfrapp's icy, synthetic take on glam feels scary and sexy at the same time, like being beaten up by a robot dominatrix. However, the best song on here is the title track—mysterious, tender, and lovely, and also my favorite flavor of yogurt.

POP TRIVIA In addition to Goldfrapp, Will Gregory leads the Will Gregory Moog Ensemble, who perform classical and film music on moogs and other early synths. He's also composed film scores and an opera.

ANIMAL COLLECTIVE

This band gives me cognitive dissonance. This is not because their eccentric mixtures of beats, sing-song vocals, and electronics make me feel weird, although that's true. It's because I don't know what to think about their hometown of Baltimore.

I thought Baltimore was the grim city of urban neglect unsparingly portrayed in *The Wire*. Well, suffice it to say that if the members of Animal Collective are on drugs, then they're not getting them from the corners controlled by the Barksdale crew.

Since 2000, Avey Tare, Panda Bear, Geologist, and Deakin (not the names they were born with) have recorded music that defies categorization. Is it dance music? Experimental pop? Electro? Neo-psychedelia? Sound art? Probably. The album and song titles (*Danse Manatee*, "Who Could Win A Rabbit," *Centipede Hz*) testify to the shared tastes of four men who originally bonded over their love of Pavement (see page 91). Avery Tare is the most prolific songwriter of the group but, as the name suggests, the members have recorded in various combinations under the Animal Collective banner, as well as releasing solo records. Deakin, in particular, has been absent from many of the group's albums and tours.

The only constants that can be applied to Animal Collective's music are an experimental impulse and an "anything goes" approach. The band members are multi-instrumentalists who incorporate everything, from synths, programming, and guitars to percussion, sampling, and field recordings. As their music has developed, they've paid increasing attention to vocals, including a frequent use of "stacked" vocal harmonies. This has invited comparisons with The Beach Boys. Thorin Klosowski of Denver's *Westworld* magazine memorably compared their music to listening to "two Beach Boys records at the same time." Indeed, the band recorded their album, *Painting With* (2016), in Studio 3 at EastWest Studios, where Brian Wilson recorded *Pet Sounds*. The record kicks off with ultimate earworm "FloriDada." In 2018 Animal Collective released an audiovisual album *Tangerine Reef*, a collaborative artwork with marine biology art group Coral Morphologic.

TOP ALBUM *Merriweather Post Pavilion* (2009) Named after a venue in Columbia, Maryland, this is one of Animal Collective's most pleasingly varied albums. Built to a large extent from samples, it takes you on an hour-long sonic ramble, from the choral euphoria of "My Girls," through the dreamy haziness of "Bluish," to the manic dance rhythms of album-closer "Brother Sport."

POP TRIVIA As well as using made-up names, the band used to perform wearing masks, wigs, and makeup. These days they have ditched the costumes, but Geologist still wears a headlamp when performing live.

THE XX

The xx have developed a distinctive sound, whose brooding atmosphere is somehow more than the sum of its minimalist parts.

Romy Madley Croft's chiming guitar stalks Oliver Sim's skeletal bass, gently propelled by the beats of Jamie xx. The xx's music is also characterized by Croft and Sim's interweaving soulful vocals, spinning tales of romantic loss and regret. The band are equally influenced by indie bands such as The Cocteau Twins (see page 64), Joy Division (see page 50), and The Cure (see page 54) as by R&B and dance culture. But it's a woozy, somnambulant version of dance music, for when the clubs are closed and the sun's coming up, not so much chill-out as comedown music.

In the UK, the band went from unknowns to unlikely stars with the release of their eponymous debut album in 2009. People fell in love with the smoldering singles "Crystalised" and "Islands," and the album won the Mercury Music Prize that year. Songs from the album were also used extensively on television, including "Intro," which was bizarrely used in the BBC's coverage of the 2010 UK general election.

The band released their follow-up record *Coexist* in 2012. On it they resisted the temptation to add lots of instrumentation or more elaborate arrangements. If anything, *Coexist* is even sparser and more minimalistic than its predecessor, with instruments dropping out of songs for long sections. Croft and Sim's vocals occasionally duet but more often echo at a distance, chasing yet failing to meet each other, like a lovelorn version of those cartoons with characters coming in and out of multiple doors.

The xx released their third album, *I See You* in 2017. While it retains the band's signature brooding style, their dancier leanings are brought to the fore and the sound is richer, more fleshed out. Opening track "Dangerous" sounds thrillingly like the band are jamming with a band of Tudor minstrels!

In addition to his work with the band, Jamie xx has also become an in-demand DJ and remixer. He remixed the late Gil Scott-Heron's last album, released as *We're New Here* (2011), and has remixed songs for other artists,

TOP ALBUM *The xx* (2009) The debut still sounds fresh, intimate, and brave. I'm running out of ways to describe the music, as weighing it down with superfluous adjectives seems contrary to its stripped-back nature. Suffice it to say that it's beautiful stuff. Once you've basked sufficiently in its luminous afterglow, put on something rowdy and chaotic like The Pogues (see page 70).

POP TRIVIA At the Manchester International Festival in 2013, the band performed a series of legendarily intimate shows. In a specially constructed space in a secret location beneath the streets of the city, they played mere feet away from an audience of only 60 people. At the culmination of each gig the "walls" of the enclosed space lifted and moved to reveal that band and audience were, in fact, in the middle of a cavernous, empty space. The band repeated the trick at the Park Avenue Armory in New York in 2014.

including Radiohead (see page 94), Florence and the Machine, and Four Tet. In 2014 he composed a score for the contemporary ballet *Tree of Codes* at the Manchester International Festival, and in 2015 he released his solo album *In Colour*.

OUTKAST

Yes, yes, alright, Outkast had actually been going since the early 1990s, but it was in the early 2000s that they broke through to a wider audience with hit singles such as "Ms. Jackson" and "Hey Ya."

"André 3000" Benjamin and Antwan "Big Boi" Patton formed Outkast in Atlanta, Georgia, in 1992 and released their first album *Southernplayalisticadillacmuzik* in 1994. Over the space of two more albums, they experimented with musical styles, playing with sci-fi imagery and incorporating a laid-back dub vibe into their sound. André 3000, in particular, adopted an increasingly eccentric dress sense and public persona.

Their fourth album, *Stankonia* (2000), was both more inventive and commercial than their previous material, and included their breakthrough single "Ms. Jackson," a perfect example of a catchy pop chorus with innovative production. Lyrically, "Ms. Jackson" was André 3000's meditation on the breakup of his relationship with Erykah Badu, but it didn't stop her from guesting on the song "Humble Mumble" later on the album. *Stankonia* featured motormouth wordplay, wacky skits, and cartoony sound effects, although beneath the tomfoolery there are serious themes, notably racial inequality and misogyny in the American south.

Speakerboxxx/The Love Below (2003) dialed the madness up to 11. It was essentially two solo albums glued together, although both members contributed to each other's album. Big Boi's half of the equation was a hip-hop, party record

with plenty of funk and smooth R&B. André 3000's half was something else altogether. *The Love Below* was an exploration of romance and sex, featuring affectionate pastiches of styles, including MOR balladry, swing, and P-Funk. André 3000, by this stage dressed like a cartoon pimp on the golf course, presented himself as a parody of a romantic lothario. The album spawned the monster hit "Hey Ya!," which has since been scientifically proven to be the best pop song ever.

Outkast recorded one more album, the soundtrack record for their underwhelming Prohibition-era movie *Idlewild* (2006), before going on hiatus. They reformed to perform live during 2014, but there are apparently no plans to make new material as Outkast.

TOP ALBUM *The Love Below* (2003) It has got to be André 3000's half of their 2003 twofer. He raids the clichés of popular romance with glee, adopting musical styles as the ideas demand. In addition to "Hey Ya!," he marries falsetto soul with manic drum & bass and church organ on "Spread" and debates shallowness and the actual smell of flowers on "Roses."

POP TRIVIA In addition to *Idlewild*, André 3000 has appeared in several films. Bearing a not inconsiderable resemblance to the man himself, there was great excitement when he was cast in a biopic of Jimi Hendrix. Sadly, the film bombed on release and was mired in controversies about the accuracy of its depiction.

DIZZEE RASCAL

Dizzee Rascal emerged from London's underground grime scene, bursting into public awareness when his debut album *Boy in da Corner* won the UK's Mercury Music Prize in 2003.

To those of us (most of us) who had no knowledge of the grime scene, *Boy in da Corner* sounded like nothing else in 2003. The beats and samples were weird and discordant, built out of massive bouncing bass, electronic odds and ends, or cut-up vocals. Over it all rapped Dizzee Rascal, a charismatic motormouth, alternately bragging and making excuses, relaying tales of being black and poor in East London. Even to those of us (most of us) a world away from such urban deprivation, it was thrilling to hear someone rapping in an unmistakably London accent and with distinctly British wit. On his debut, he channeled a troubled youth during which he had frequent run-ins with the law and was kicked out of multiple schools. He began producing music on a school PC with the encouragement of a forward-thinking teacher.

After winning the Mercury at the age of 19, it's amazing that he didn't lose his mind. In fact, he kept it together remarkably well, concentrating on recording his follow-up album, *Showtime*, which was released in 2004. The album was as sonically adventurous as its predecessor, building tracks out of atonal hums and squeaks. On the album's second single, "Dream," Dizzee tried a more tuneful approach, rapping over a sample of Captain Sensible's cover of "Happy Talk" to hilarious effect. "Dream" also had a great video in which he rapped with puppets in the style of '50s kids' TV.

On subsequent albums Dizzee moved further away from his grime beginnings, embracing a more commercial dance sound and working with mainstream dance producers Calvin Harris and Armand Van Helden (on stupid but fun smash hit "Bonkers"). His fifth album, imaginatively titled *The Fifth* (2013), featured wearying collaborations with Jessie J, Robbie Williams, and will.i.am.

In 2017 he released *Raskit*, a partial return to the more ferocious, sound of his early music. Stepping up to prove himself in the contemporary landscape of next-generation grime stars such as Skepta and Stormzy, Dizzee performs dextrous, tumbling raps, delivering unsentimental descriptions of his London youth.

TOP ALBUM *Boy in da Corner* (2003) This still sounds remarkably fresh, brimming with the boisterous charm and creative glee of its young creator. It's full of great tracks, but two highlights are the thrilling "Fix Up, Look Sharp" and "Jus' a Rascal," with its cheeky choral refrain.

POP TRIVIA In 2003, in the same week that *Boy in da Corner* was released, Dizzee Rascal was stabbed six times in Ayia Napa. This was apparently the result of feuding between rival London crews. Ouch. Don't take your beef on holiday, kids.

CHAPTER FIVE

THE Twenty-Tens STAGE

FEATURING THE FOLLOWING ARTISTS:

LUCIUS

white denim

JANELLE MONÁE

CATE LE BON

Courtney Barnett

bon iver

Tame Impala

FKA Twigs

ST. VINCENT

John Grant

Father John Misty

KENDRICK LAMAR

R&B ★ PSYCHEDELIA ★ FOLK ★ ELECTRO ★ ROCK ★ HIP-HOP

LUCIUS

It's possible that I've overused the word "sassy" in this book. I should have reserved it only for Lucius.

The band are built around the twin vocals of Jess Wolfe and Holly Laessig, whose big and yes, sassy, voices join together, at times in supportive harmony, at others in double-tracked unison. Their brassy sound is reminiscent of the girl groups of the 1960s and the female Motown groups, but also dips into blues, country, and '80s pop. Visually, Wolfe and Laessig draw attention to their dazzling vocal unity by dressing identically and sporting matching haircuts. The striking image is accentuated by the fact that one is tall (Laessig) and the other is short (Wolfe). Live, they perform facing each other and side-on to the audience, singing into each other's faces while playing a variety of mini-keyboards and percussion. Further back are drummer Dan Molad and guitarist Peter Lalish.

Lucius released their first album, *Songs From The Bromley House*, in 2009, but it was their follow-up that brought them to wider attention. *Wildewoman* (2013) is a compelling collection of instant-classic pop songs, ranging from full-throated (and sassy) celebration to bluesy lament. The title track is a term that Wolfe and Laessig coined for fearsome, strong women. They released their third album, *Good Grief*, in 2016. It's less bluesy than its predecessor, drawing its inspiration from the '80s rather than the '60s. Wonky synths, drum machines, and treated guitar underpin the vocals. It sounds more processed, more compressed, and yet also more emotional, at times bordering on hysteria. The drum-machine rocker "Born Again Teen" is reminiscent of St. Vincent (see page 150) and "Almighty Gosh" shows the healthy influence of Kate Bush in her '80s prime (see page 44). "Gone Insane" starts off with icy resentment and concludes with a genuinely scary vocal performance.

In 2018 Lucius released *Nudes*, an intimate album of largely acoustic songs, comprising new material, reworked songs from their back catalogue and covers of Gerry Rafferty and Tame Impala (see page 148). It's final track, traditional belter "Goodnight Irene", is a duet with Pink Floyd's Roger Walters, with whom Wolfe and Laessig have toured as backing singers.

TOP ALBUM *Wildewoman* (2013) It's fair to say that there's an embarrassment of riches on this record. "Turn it Around" is the sassiest of the sassy (last time, I promise). It's all in the way the girls shout "...hah!" "Go Home" features some fantastic blues slide guitar and a storming vocal performance, while "How Loud Your Heart Gets" is like the great Wilson Phillips song that the '80s forgot. My favorite is "Genevieve," which only appears on the European edition of the album. Sorry America!

POP TRIVIA Lucius have an unlikely celebrity fan in anti-austerity economist and columnist Paul Krugman. He has written about the band in his *The New York Times* column and apparently regularly attends their New York gigs. I look forward to Lucius' next album *Fiscal Stimulus Policy*.

white denim

White Denim are the perfect combination of brawn and brains. From the musical city of Austin, Texas, they look like handsome hillbillies, good ol' boys in Levi's and denim shirts, who you'd expect to find hanging around a trailer park. Indeed, they recorded their early material in drummer Josh Block's trailer. I think White Denim's a brilliant name for a band; my wife thinks it's possibly the worst name ever.

White Denim offer a frenetic but oddball take on rock music, combining muscular garage rock riffs with more cerebral experiments in rhythm and structure. They often sound like Thin Lizzy gone Krautrock, but their music also incorporates psychedelia, punk, jazz, country, tropicana, and soul influences.

Their early records were self-produced and sold at shows. Originally a power trio of Block (drums), James Petralli (lead vocals, guitar), and Steve Terebecki (vocals, bass), they added second guitarist Austin Jenkins to the line-up in 2010, so producing a beefier sound and more complicated guitar arrangements. Their songs frequently feature virtuosic guitar solos and they are famed as a live act for their extended jams and improvised wig-outs. The first recorded output to feature the four-man line-up was 2010's *Last Day of Summer*, initially released for free through their website. It was a collection of old songs and extras recorded by the band while they made an official studio album.

That album, *D* (2011), demonstrated their sonic power, but also their stylistic breadth, from the frantic riffing of "Back At The Farm" to the gentle country trot of "Keys." White Denim described their follow-up, 2013's *Corsicana Lemonade*, as their "barbecue record" and it was accordingly warm and mellow, with big bluesy riffs and fuzzy guitars. "Pretty Green" recalled the 1970s good-time rock of bands such as Free, while "At Night In Dreams" made explicit the Thin Lizzy comparisons.

The next album, *Stiff* (2016), was recorded by a new line-up, following the departure of Austin and Block. The band went back to the frantic sound of their early material, embracing the dumb joy of raucous rock music. As Petralli said, "We thought, what's the fundamental thing that made us want to get into a van and quit our terrible jobs and start this whole thing in the first place? And it was loud, fast-playing rock 'n' roll."

Not known for twiddling their thumbs, White Denim have released three studio albums and a live album since 2016. *Performance* (2018) is the band at their most fun, stuffed to the gills with chunky riffs and catchy tunes,. In 2019 they put out *Side Effects*, a sporadically brilliant album of worked up cast-offs from their vaults, *and* a killer live album, *In Person*. In 2020 they responded to the cancellation of tours caused by the Covid 19 breakout by deciding to write and record an album, *World as a Waiting Room* in 30 days in their home studio.

TOP ALBUM *D* (2011) The band's earlier albums are full of great moments, but *D* is where it all comes together. The band demonstrate the eclectic range of their influences and everything they try their hand at comes off, often morphing styles and time signatures in the space of a song. Opening track "It's Him!" is a good example—it starts with salvos of guitar and barreling drums, then dives into atmospheric swamp rock, before switching again to syncopated guitar lines that mix funk with the folk rock of Pentangle. On "Is and Is and Is," Petralli momentarily transforms into Ian Astbury of The Cult.

POP TRIVIA It's no accident that *Corsicana Lemonade* (2013) shows off the band's soul influence. Around this time, Austin and Block began working with Texan soul sensation Leon Bridges. They played on, co-wrote, and produced his debut album *Coming Home* (2015). Simultaneously, Petralli, under the pseudonym of Bop English, made a solo album called *Constant Bop* (2015), which sounds, not unreasonably, like White Denim.

WE'VE BEEN ASKED TO PLAY AT FABRIC.

OH YEAH? WHO ELSE IS PLAYING?

SUEDE, ELASTICA, FELT, CORDUROY, ERM...DENIM.

THEY WANT US TO GO DOUBLE-DENIM?!

TELL THEM WE'LL ONLY DO IT IF WE CAN PLAY AGADOO WITH BLACK LACE.

JANELLE MONÁE

Mainstream R&B and hip-hop are often grimly down to earth, stroking their obsessions with sex and material success. Janelle Monáe is an inspiring antidote to all of this, creating concept albums that, in the great tradition of sci-fi, tackle contemporary social concerns through their fantastical metaphors. And while her material has become increasingly sexually explicit, it is so in a way that celebrates personal freedom and experimentation.

Musically, Monáe keeps one polished spat in R&B, but ventures into an eclectic range of styles that includes soul, hip-hop, psychedelic rock, funk, classical, and Broadway musicals. In her fondness for a wacky, sci-fi concept she harks back to Bowie and Ziggy (see page 10), but also the Afro-futurism of George Clinton (see page 36).

Born and raised in Kansas City, Monáe was influenced as a child by *The Wizard of Oz* and identified early on with Dorothy Gale, that other Kansas girl whose imagination took her to a fantastical land. She began making music after moving to Atlanta, where she befriended local musical heroes Outkast, another hip-hop outfit with a love of a bizarre concept (see page 136). She sang on Outkast's soundtrack album *Idlewild* (2006) and Big Boi later recommended her to Sean "Puffy/Puff Daddy/P. Diddy/Seany Poo" Combs who signed her to his Bad Boy Records.

Monáe self-released the first part of her *Metropolis Suite* in 2007 but, after signing her up, Bad Boy Records re-released it as *Metropolis: Suite I (The Chase)* in 2008. The seven-track EP introduced Monáe's alter ego Cindi Mayweather, an android from 2719 ad who is forced to go on the run after falling in love with a human. Suites II and III became her debut album, *The ArchAndroid*, released by Bad Boy in 2010. This record continued the story, with Cindi Mayweather now a messianic figure for the future society's androids. Conceptually, her project drew heavily on the writings of science-fiction author Philip K. Dick and Fritz Lang's iconic film *Metropolis*. The album cover shows Monáe styled after *Metropolis'* robotic anti-heroine Maria.

Her follow-up album *The Electric Lady* (2013) continued to explore themes of social and personal development through the imagery of androids and future utopias/dystopias. It was peppered with radio DJ skits alluding to Cindi Mayweather's android revolution and had a noticeably more star-studded cast than its predecessor, featuring contributions from Prince (see page 60), Erykah Badu, and Solange Knowles.

In 2018 she released her most ambitious project yet. *Dirty Computer*, the album, is newly direct in its celebration of pansexual freedom and hedonism, dissecting the power structures of American, white, straight culture over glossy synths, trap beats, and sultry Prince-style riffs. Monáe ditched her signature black and white "uniform" for this technicolor album, and her broadened stylistic spectrum is referenced in the song "Pynk". The song's provocative and wittily clitoral video is one part of the accompanying *Dirty Computer* film, which really ups the sci-fi dystopian ante. The "Emotion Picture" is a polyamorous and pansexual love story set in a homophobic and racist police state that punishes non-comformity. Within this linking narrative, the individual songs are memories in the mind of Monáe's character, Jane 57821, whose brain is being scrubbed by evil scientists. Subtle it ain't, but it's hugely enjoyable—progressive, accomplished, camp, and ridiculous in equal measure.

TOP ALBUM *The ArchAndroid* (2010) This is insanely ambitious and great fun. It's a smorgas-cyborg of musical retro-futurism. "Sir Greendown" is a lovely ode to Cindi's human lover, the hit single "Tightrope" is a slice of swinging retro-funk featuring Outkast's Big Boi, and "Oh Maker" is like an electro-funk-chanson distillation of *Blade Runner* in which the android questions the intentions of her creator.

POP TRIVIA Monáe is also an accomplished actress. She has appeared in *Hidden Figures*, *Harriet*, and the Oscar-winning *Moonlight*, and starred in the horror movie *Antebellum*. She also lent her voice to a character in *Rio 2*. I was forced to watch *Rio 2* when babysitting my niece and nephew. I forgive you, Janelle.

CATE LE BON

Cate Le Bon is a Welsh singer-songwriter, who plays off-kilter songs with surreal poetic lyrics sung in a distinctive, Nico-esque voice.

Le Bon first came to exposure supporting Gruff Rhys on tour and contributing vocals to his 2008 concept album *Neon Neon*. Her first album, *Me Oh My* (2009), featured folky songs that are reminiscent of the lighter side of The Velvet Underground, embroidered with weird electronics, fuzz guitar, and sinister organ. 2012's album, *Cyrk,* was a rowdier affair, full of clanging guitar and cheesy organ, mixing garage rock with psych-folk and the odd hint of country.

Le Bon moved to LA in 2013 and recorded her third album with producer Noah Georgeson. *Mug Museum* (2013) is lean and stripped back, and its angular, wandering guitar parts bear the influence of New York punks Television. *Mug Museum*'s ponderings on relationships were in part caused by the death of Le Bon's grandmother and, although the album title sounds like surreal whimsy, it was actually a phrase that her father coined to describe the unwashed teacups in her bedroom. Her fourth album, *Crab Day* (2016), pursues the garage sound of *Mug Museum* into weirder straits, with bursts of saxophone, glockenspiel flourishes, and repetitive passages of plodding piano, like an acid-tinged Chas and Dave. The sax is back on Le Bon's 2019 record, *Reward* but it's been cranked up. Woven from plaintive piano with frequent skronks of foghorn saxophone, these are wobbly torch songs of longing and regret. I saw Le Bon live when this came out, and as good as the album is, live her voice soared over the music.

TOP ALBUM *Mug Museum* (2013) This is pitched at the perfect spot between Le Bon's pop and avant-garde sensibilities. It opens with glorious companion pieces "I Can't Help You" and "Are You With Me Now?," both different, yet defined by gorgeous melodies and clever, spidery guitar parts. Other highlights of the album are her duet with Perfume Genius, "I Think I Knew," and the uncharacteristically mournful title track, which features just Le Bon's voice, piano, sax, and a creaky chair.

POP TRIVIA To promote *Crab Day*, Le Bon released a short film of the same name, directed by the artist Phil Collins (no, not *that* Phil Collins). It featured her and a troupe of strangely dressed dancers performing interpretative dance in a Berlin housing estate.

Courtney Barnett

Courtney Barnett slouched onto the scene in 2013 with the global release of her *A Sea of Split Peas* double EP collection and effortlessly established herself as the queen of observational slacker rock.

Barnett speak-sings in her distinctive Aussie drawl, assembling her thoughts into conversational monologs over woozily strummed jams, often accompanied by a hint of bluesy slide guitar. Her lyrics incorporate wordplay and she has a fondness for a crap pun, as in her early single "Avant Gardener." You can imagine having a few enjoyable drinks with Courtney. In addition to "Avant Gardener," *A Sea of Split Peas* featured "History Eraser," which related a surreal and teasingly erotic daydream over a rocking riff, and subtler, more atmospheric tracks such as "Anonymous Club" and "Canned Tomatoes (Whole)."

Barnett made her full album debut in 2015 with *Sometimes I Sit and Think, and Sometimes I Just Sit*. She managed to wring a surprising number of moods from the talky-singing-plus-guitars formula, from the T-Rex-ish stomp of "Elevator Operator" to the strung-out feel of "Depreston." Her next album was a collaboration with American rocker Kurt Vile, *Lotta Sea Lice* (2017). It was a marriage made in slacker heaven, her laid back intonation matched by his practically horizontal vocals. The next album, *Tell Me How You Really Feel* (2018) sticks close to her poppy, slouch-rock formula, with winking but confessional titles such as "Crippling Self Doubt and a General Lack of Confidence".

TOP ALBUM *Sometimes I Sit and Think, and Sometimes I Just Sit* (2015) Sometimes... is stuffed full of catchy, laconic pop songs with lyrics of deadpan wit, ranging from righteous rage at fakery on the storming "Pedestrian at Best" to insomniac metaphysical speculation on "An Illustration of Loneliness." Along the way she shakes her head at house prices and wonders about the health benefits of organic vegetables.

POP TRIVIA "Avant Gardener's" tale of gardening going badly wrong is apparently based on real events. Barnett was laid out by an anaphylactic shock while doing a spot of pruning and was rushed to hospital. .

Like the Fleet Foxes (see page 126), Bon Iver is the sound of beardy Americans singing in close harmonies. But whereas Fleet Foxes' songs are intricately constructed pieces of folk engineering, Bon Iver's songs are stripped back and sketchy. On debut album, *For Emma, Forever Ago* (2007), it often sounds as if Justin Vernon is sat next to you singing in your ear.

Like Tame Impala (see page 148), Bon Iver is really a one-man band in all but name. Justin Vernon began recording what would be his breakthrough album in a cabin in Wisconsin in the winter of 2006. It's fair to say that he was going through something of a rocky period, having lost both his band *and* girlfriend but gained a nasty liver infection. He left North Carolina and drove back to Wisconsin, where he hid from the world at his dad's hunting cabin. At first he binge-watched DVDs of *Northern Exposure*—the name Bon Iver comes from a mis-transcription of "bon hiver" (French for "good winter") from an episode of the show—but, once he had exhausted the possibilities of Alaskan, televisual magic-realism, he began writing and recording songs.

For Emma, Forever Ago is suffused with the beautiful melancholy of winter. The songs are like nagging thoughts of regret and doubt, sad memories that drift across your mind's eye. The arrangements are fragile and minimal, often just a strummed guitar or two and lots of space, like fields of virgin snow. Vernon's multi-tracked falsetto is always top in the mix, sometimes just one pure line of melody, at other times singing harmony in virtual choirs. Having recorded the album almost by accident, Vernon regarded it as a demo to attract record company investment but was persuaded by friends to self-release *For Emma, Forever Ago* in 2007. This version attracted the attention of label Jagjaguwar, who signed Bon Iver and re-released the album the following year.

The album became a word-of-mouth hit and Vernon recruited musicians to play the songs live and then to record the follow-up. *Bon Iver, Bon Iver* (2011) is as musically expansive as the debut was insular. Brass, saxophone, pedal steel, and banjo drift in and out of the moody arrangements, although the soaring falsetto still presides over all.

Bon Iver's next album, *22, A Million* (2016) left the beardy folk woodsman image in the dust. Guitars, banjos, and saxophones are still audible but everything has been put through the electronic wringer, broken apart and stitched together in strange shapes. The most prominent instrument is Vernon's voice but this too has been discombobulated and deformed, frequently autotuned and roboticized.

2019's *i,i* is a similarly tricksy beast, continuing Bon Iver's playful attitude to production and song structure. The electronically treated vocal yelps of "iMi" recall the title track of Radiohead's Kid A (see page 94), but there are less experimental moments, such as the gospel-influenced "U (Man Like)" and the euphoric "Naeem". Vernon reminds me of Sufjan Stevens in his insistence on pushing beyond the limits of his initial folk-pop successes, but if I'm honest I'm not quite sure he has Sufjan's songwriting chops.

TOP ALBUM *For Emma, Forever Ago* (2007) This album is a thing of subtle, wintry beauty. Its gentle, strummed guitars lull and beguile with folk and country rhythms. Vernon's lyrics are confessional, yet ambiguous, and couched in poetic imagery. The breakthrough single "Skinny Love" has a disarming directness, while "Team" concludes with some enthusiastic whistling. There should be more whistling in pop music.

POP TRIVIA Justin Vernon has worked with a number of other acts as musician or producer. He contributed vocals to Kanye West's "love-it-or-hate-it" 2010 album, *My Beautiful Dark Twisted Fantasy* (see page 130), and produced *If I Was*, the second album by terrific UK folk-pop group The Staves.

WHAT LURKS IN THE...

Tame Impala

The music of Tame Impala is the most psychedelic thing to come out of Australia since the "Bouncer's Dream" episode of Aussie soap opera _Neighbours_, in which a pet dog dreamed of his own wedding.

Tame Impala is the project of Perth musician Kevin Parker, who writes and records most of the music himself, augmented by other Perth musicians when playing live. His songwriting is steeped in the psychedelic rock of the 1960s and '70s, and boasts acid-fried vocals and waves of fuzzy guitar, treated drums, and synths.

Parker began recording as Tame Impala in 2007 and put out two well-received EPs and the 2009 single "Sundown Syndrome," before releasing debut album, _Innerspeaker_ (2010). Parker played most of the instruments, with occasional help from Jay Watson and Dom Simper, and also produced the album himself, with engineering assistance from Tim Holmes of Death in Vegas. The album was mixed by Flaming Lips' producer Dave Fridmann, a man well-versed in neo-psychedelic sounds. Parker told _The Quietus_ (ace music website, FYI) that the record's title was derived from the idea of accessing music as he heard it in his head—"if someone plugged a stereo into your brain they'd be able to hear it."

Tame Impala's next album, _Lonerism_ (2012), was recorded in Perth, on tour, and in France. While he again wrote and recorded much of the material himself, _Lonerism_ also featured songs that he co-wrote with Jay Watson, including the singles "Elephant" and "Apocalypse Dreams." Heavily influenced by Todd Rundgren, the album has a poppier feel than the debut, relying less on guitars and more on wobbly synths. Lyrically, _Lonerism_ dwells on feelings of isolation, a theme that is emphasized by the album cover which shows a cool party behind a closed gate.

The third album, _Currents_ (2015), sounds less like rock and more like electro-soul or even dance music. Though Parker has resisted the description of _Currents_ as a break-up record, it was at least partially inspired by his split from French singer Melody Prochet and its lyrics dwell on personal transformation.

Tame Impala's latest album, _The Slow Rush_ (2020) continues this move away from rock into contemporary pop. There's precious little crunchy guitar here but waves of pulsing synth, dancey keyboards, and soulful, honeyed vocals. It has incorporated stylistic tricks from R&B, MOR pop, and hip-hop.

TOP ALBUM _Lonerism_ (2012) Both more experimental and accessible than the band's debut, this album features expansive synths, pop melodies, and field recordings taped while on tour. If _Innerspeaker_ sounds like Cream and Hendrix, _Lonerism_ is more like the trippier parts of _Sgt. Pepper_. "Apocalypse Dreams" sounds like Motown if someone spiked the musicians, "Feels Like We Only Go Backwards" will have you floating round the room, and "Elephant" barrels toward you on a Sabbath-esque riff before taking a side road into the synth store.

POP TRIVIA In addition to Tame Impala, Parker has worked with bands such as Pond and his ex-girlfriend's band, Melody's Echo Chamber, and contributed to Mark Ronson's _Uptown Funk_.

FKA Twigs

FKA Twigs is as much a dancer as a musician as a producer as a video artist. She collaborates with producers, choreographers, designers, and stylists on each release, creating music perfectly synched with the video and her costumes.

Born Tahliah Debrett Barnett in Gloucestershire, at the age of 17 FKA Twigs moved to London, where she worked as a back-up dancer for pop performers, including Kylie, Jessie J, and Plan B. However, inspired by Billie Holiday and Siouxsie and the Banshees (among many other influences), she had more ambitious music in mind. She released *EP1* through Bandcamp in 2012, while its follow-up, *EP2*, was released by Young Turks in 2013. Twigs made a video for all eight songs on the two EPs, releasing them gradually through her YouTube channel. Among the startling images were those for "Papi Pacify," in which a muscular man repeatedly pushed his fingers into Twigs' mouth, and "Water Me," in which her crying eyes gradually grew to cartoon proportions.

FKA Twigs has a lithe, dancer's body and looks like Frida Kahlo made into a doll. She exploits this plastic, doll-like appearance in the aforementioned "Water Me" video, as well as in the arresting cover of her album *LP1* (2014) and the later video for "I'm Your Doll." Her music has been described as alternative R&B, but is equally reminiscent of trip-hop artists such as Tricky and Massive Attack (see page 83), as well as the skewed soundscapes of Aphex Twin (see page 99). It generally features off-kilter beats, ominous echoes, and strange clangs, including sounds recorded from everyday life. "How's That" and "Water Me" from *EP2* both include what sounds like a clock going berserk. Twigs' vocals are breathy and choral, with occasional dips into a bluesier register. She often builds pulses out of her sampled vocals, reminiscent of Laurie Anderson's "O Superman!"

In 2014, she released her first album, *LP1,* whose moody soundscapes varied from deconstructed R&B to ethereal trance music. She released three typically provocative videos from the album. The frankly sexual "Two Weeks" portrayed her as a giant, Cleopatra-like queen pouring golden liquid over dancing mini-Twigs. "Pendulum" showed her in various S&M contortions, bound by her own hair, and in "Video Girl" she sang to a prisoner on death row as he was being executed. *LP1* was nominated for the Mercury Prize in the UK.

In 2015 she released a five-track EP called *M3LL155X,* but pronounced "Mellissa." The songs were like R&B beamed in from some parallel world, possibly via that creepy TV in the film *Poltergeist*. The sense of them being a suite of songs was emphasized by the video directed by Twigs, featuring four of the tracks. Memorably, it showed Twigs as a blow-up sex doll and later giving birth to multicolored ribbons, as if performing a bizarre magician's trick.

In 2017 she split from fiancé Robert Pattinson, and in 2018 revealed that she had undergone surgery to remove fibroids from her uterus. Her second full-length album, *Magdalene* (2019) sounds appropriately like she has been put through the wringer but crucially that she has emerged strong and in full command of her considerable talents.

TOP ALBUM *Magdalene* (2019) Her relationship with R-Patz propelled Twigs to a new level of fame. Having been chewed up by the tabloid celebrity machine, on her second album she identifies with Mary Magdalene as a feminist cultural icon whose image has been used and abused by the patriarchy. *Magdalene* is an intense and earnest listen, in part a break-up album, in part a brave statement of survival. Twigs' ethereal vocals float over music that fizzes and pops, shifting over skittish beats. The opening track "thousand eyes" starts like religious choral music, before darkening opressively. "home with you" blossoms into trilling flutes and a full jazz band. The vocals and arrangement on "fallen alien" consciously invoke the spirit of Kate Bush (see page 44), and "day-bed" is a spooky little song with a lyric that charmingly mentions friendly fruit flies.

POP TRIVIA In 2015, Twigs spent seven days at the Manchester International Festival, constructing seven new dance pieces, one a day, in front of a studio audience. The pieces were performed at the end of her residency and images, gifs, and audio from the process were shared on Tumblr.

ST. VINCENT

Annie Clark, aka St. Vincent, is an innovative and eccentric songwriter. Her songs incorporate all sorts of styles, from rock to jazz and electronic dance music, but are often characterized by her brittle guitar and cut-glass vocal performances.

Before releasing her own records, St. Vincent played with cult pop cultists The Polyphonic Spree and was a member of Sufjan Stevens' touring band (see page 107). Her first album, *Marry Me* (2007), was a bold debut, featuring experimental arrangements and contributions from Bowie's jazz piano maestro Mike Garson. Returning from a lengthy tour, she began work on her second album. To kick-start her tour-frazzled brain, she watched classic movies, including Disney films and *The Wizard of Oz*, in some cases composing music to scenes with the sound turned down before writing lyrics. The resulting album, *Actor* (2009), features rich string arrangements and a spooky, fairytale vibe. Her next album, *Strange Mercy* (2011), was recorded over a workaholic month in Seattle and featured more personal, yet often ambiguous, lyrics about emotional conflict, sexual desire, and depression.

Clark named her fourth album simply *St. Vincent* (2014), a sign of the confidence she had gained in her musical persona. Whereas *Strange Mercy* was emotionally raw and introverted, *St. Vincent* was an extrovert record, with more emphasis on electronic and dance rhythms. Clark described it as "a party record you could play at a funeral." Highlights include "Rattlesnake," based on a close encounter in the desert and the funky, social media critique "Digital Witness." Her increasing self-confidence was also evidenced in her new look, her frizzy hair dyed silver like a sci-fi ice queen. For live shows, she devised "conveyor belt" choreography with band member Toko Yasuda and effortlessly played solo guitar while writhing down a pink, plastic ziggurat.

In 2017 St. Vincent released her fifth album, *Masseduction*. The cover shows what appears to be a still from a demented '80s aerobics class, the colors turned up to eye-bleeding saturation. The music picks up from where the previous album left off, all harsh angles, fuzz guitars and programmed synthetic drums. She sings of sex and submission but these songs are detached, glassy-eyed, a strain of paranoia running beneath the pop sheen. One of the most arresting tracks (and the title of the accompanying tour) is called "Fear the Future".

In addition to her solo albums, St. Vincent recorded *Love This Giant* (2012) with David Byrne (see page 34). It's a brilliant collection of art-funk songs with New Orleans brass arrangements, which Clark and Byrne composed gradually, swapping files over email..

TOP ALBUM *Strange Mercy* (2011) This is full of oblique poetry and dazzling, inventive arrangements. The lyrics touch on sexual politics, personal regret, and emotional vulnerability. The music is sinuous and unpredictable, moving from the woozy, Hollywood strings of "Cruel" to the trip-hop balladry of the title track, "Strange Mercy."

POP TRIVIA St. Vincent took her name from Nick Cave's song "There She Goes, My Beautiful World" (see page 96). Among descriptions of famous authors and their writing habits, it mentions Welsh poet Dylan Thomas' alcoholic death in St. Vincent's Hospital, New York.

ST. VINCENT'S HOUSE

DIGITAL WITNESS™ SECURITY SYSTEM

John Grant

John Grant has an excellent beard, a delicious baritone voice, and a fine line in wittily bleak lyrics, alternately self-lacerating and outwardly hostile. His moody songs openly explore his troubled history and emotional turmoil, but often through pop cultural metaphors drawn from movies and books.

Grant released his first solo album, *Queen of Denmark*, in 2010 but before that he had been lead singer of The Czars. He recorded *Queen of Denmark* with the folk rock band Midlake, who had persuaded him to make a solo album after seeing him in concert. Grant has spoken since of how Midlake saved his life, by helping to lift him out of a period of deep depression and substance abuse.

The music on *Queen of Denmark* is stately and dramatic, Grant's lovely croon carried along by folk rock with orchestral flourishes. Many of the songs dwell on lost love, depression, and his ambiguous feelings toward society, but it's not all doom and gloom. Grant is as much Randy Newman as Leonard Cohen, and he peppers his songs with witty bon mots and amusingly offbeat comparisons. "Sigourney Weaver" compares his existential despair to the experiences of Weaver in *Aliens* and Winona Ryder in *Dracula*. In general, his lyrics veer between elegy and angry confrontation. Grant loves a withering put-down and gratuitous swearing, and *Queen of Denmark* features plenty of both, accompanied by scathing criticisms of mainstream, heterosexual masculinity. In particular, "Jesus hates Faggots" takes on religious persecution of homosexuals and then broadens out to a general attack on religious intolerance of all stripes. Grant grew up gay in a strict, religious family in Colorado and became estranged from his family after coming out. His anger toward the cultural prejudices that saddled him with years of self-hatred and suicidal impulses is palpable.

Grant moved to Reykjavík, Iceland, and began working on his second album, *Pale Green Ghosts* (2013), with Birgir Pórarinsson of Icelandic dance group GusGus. Whereas his first album was colored by Midlake's soft rock sound, his second tends toward skittish electro with cinematic strings. The phrase "Pale Green Ghosts" comes from his memory of the olive trees that lined the I-25 highway near his home in Parker, Colorado. "Black Belt" is a great big "fuck you" in electronic form and "GMF" is perhaps the ultimate John Grant song, featuring a beautiful, elegiac melody, self-lacerating sarcasm, outward hostility, and swearing topped off with a reference to Richard Burton's corpse. "Ernest Borgnine" alludes to Grant's HIV diagnosis and former drug habits, and combines electronic beats with jazz saxophone in a way that looks forward three years to Bowie's *Blackstar* (see page 10). Sinead O'Connor provides backing vocals on three tracks, including the final song "Glacier." "Glacier" moves along at a stately pace appropriate to its name and its dramatic orchestral ending leads directly into what he did next. In 2014, Grant recorded a live album with the BBC Philharmonic, featuring orchestral arrangements of songs from his first two albums.

He released his third album in 2015. *Grey Tickles, Black Pressure* was recorded in Texas and written by an increasingly grounded Grant, now happily settled in Reykjavík. The album opens and concludes with readings from 1 Corinthians: "Love is patient, love is kind..." but thankfully he still found plenty of emotional grist and scores to settle.

His latest album, *Love is Magic* (2018) is a beguiling tour of the territory Grant has mapped out over his career thus far. There is bubbling '80s pop ("Preppy Boy" and "He's Got His Mother's Hips"), glacial synths ("Tempest"), foul-mouthed insults ("Diet Gum" and erm, track 5) as well as moody ballads and woozy, hard won romance (the title tack).

TOP ALBUM *Grey Tickles, Black Pressure* (2015) This mixes the electronic sound of his sophomore album with the piano-driven torch songs of his debut. The title track ups the mordant comedy to 11, mentioning hemorrhoid medicine commercials, children with cancer, and an agricultural accident that befell Grant's uncle. "Snug Slacks" sounds like a gay re-write of Beck's *Midnite Vultures*, while "Down Here" is a softly strummed ode to mortality and futility, with a mean bass clarinet solo. "Voodoo Doll" starts off like The Magnetic Fields, then morphs into Michael Jackson, and "Disappointing" is a rare foray into positivity, but crucially approaches happiness through the back door.

POP TRIVIA John Grant can speak at least four languages in addition to English. The title *Grey Tickles, Black Pressure* is derived from an Icelandic phrase for middle age and a Turkish phrase for a nightmare. Since settling in Iceland, he has contributed to the national culture by co-writing their 2014 Eurovision song, performed by the band Pollapönk.

Father John Misty

In 2012 Josh Tillman left the Fleet Foxes (see page 126), to concentrate on producing music under his new moniker, Father John Misty. "You know, you can only put a narcissist behind a drum-kit for so long," he told *Clash Music*.

His big spiritual epiphany (apparently involving some hallucinogens) was that he was and always had been "a kind of smart-ass." He decided to write songs that reveled in his egocentric faults, paradoxically as the character Father John Misty, an untrustworthy but charismatic crooner of folk and country-tinged soul.

Father John Misty's first album, *Fear Fun* (2012), still owes something to the folk harmonies of the Fleet Foxes, but leans in the direction of bar-room ballads and ostentatious torch songs. Lyrically, *Fear Fun* is full of self-deprecating descriptions of male failings and bad behavior, dramatizing Tillman's transformation from fey singer-songwriter to pretentious visionary, as on the hilarious "I'm Writing A Novel."

Father John Misty released his second album, the sumptuous *I Love You, Honey Bear*, in 2015 to great acclaim. Tillman, who clearly enjoys the "boxes within boxes" dislocation of his artistic conceit, has described it as a concept album about J. Tillman and, indeed, its fourth song was called "The Night That Josh Tillman Came To Our Apt." Musically, it's a gorgeous mixture of folk and country, orchestrated with lush strings, mariachi trumpets, and tremolo guitar, with a brief foray into electro.

His third album, *Pure Comedy* (2017) was not so much a state-of-the-nation as state-of-the-species record. The lengthy opening title track sketches a brief history of humanity as evolutionarily compromised mammals who have built a corrupt, hypocritical society as a self-deluding survival mechanism. The final track, "In Twenty Years or So" speculates that this whole charade might be about to collapse. The centerpiece of this hugely ambitious album is "Leaving LA", a knowingly self-indulgent 13-minute epic which starts out recalling Tillman's pre-Misty earnest folk stylings but evolves into lush orchestration.

God's Favorite Customer (2018), followed quickly on the heels of *Pure Comedy*, and in contrast is a relatively straightforward collection of ten songs, loosely themed around Tillman's apparent breakdown and dissolute time spent living in a hotel. The mood is characteristically arch and gloomy, but from the sardonic darkness emerge moments of beauty and emotional truth, as on suicidal lament "Please Don't Die". My two-year old looked at the moody picture of Father John Misty on the album cover and said "hmm, he sad".

TOP ALBUM *I Love You Honey Bear* (2015) This is a mordantly hilarious, warts-and-all confession of bad behavior and unkind thoughts, wrapped up as a seductive come-on. The record is also, perhaps somewhat surprisingly, a heartfelt tribute to Tillman's wife, a love letter from a cynic who isn't sure he believes in love. It's peppered with wry admissions of dysfunction (the title song and "The Ideal Husband"), and "The Night That Josh Tillman Came To Our Apt." contains some fantastically mean put-downs.

POP TRIVIA Father John Misty loves winding up the press. In 2015, he began recording a cover album of Ryan Adams' cover album of Taylor Swift's *1989*, only in the style of The Velvet Underground. He then removed this work-in-progress from his Soundcloud page, telling journalists that Lou Reed had appeared to him in a dream and told him to stop. He also claimed to have had a religious experience while watching a Taylor Swift concert in Melbourne, under the influence of a heavy dose of LSD.

KENDRICK LAMAR

Is Kendrick Lamar the best rapper in the world right now? Quite possibly. His tracks are virtuoso displays of rapping, their sophisticated interrogations of contemporary America backed by musical arrangements that are influenced by jazz and funk.

Named after The Temptations' Eddie Kendricks, Kendrick Lamar Duckworth grew up in Compton, California, made infamous by original gangsta-rappers N.W.A. Indeed, his early heroes were Dr. Dre and Tupac Shakur. Lamar's style takes the laid-back, groove-based blueprint of West Coast rap, but manages a greater lyrical and musical sophistication, zooming out to a broader consideration of politics and society.

He began producing mix tapes and performing under the name of K-Dot. *Overly Dedicated* (2010) was officially still a mix tape, but was well on the way to his later concept albums. "Ignorance Is Bliss," in particular, showed the ambiguity he felt toward the gangsta rap image, opening with the plea "Lord forgive me" and then punctuating its violent boasts with the self-critical refrain "Ignorance is bliss." His first album proper, 2011's *Section.80*, was his first attempt at shaping a whole record around a concept, in this case the societal problems of his apathetic generation, born in Reagan's dysfunctional 1980s. Its final track and lead-off single "HiiiPower" was a paranoid and revolutionary critique of contemporary America, but also one that attempted to salvage a philosophy of personal empowerment through Lamar's "HiiiPower" concept. The three "i"s symbolize "heart, honor, and respect." "i" as a totem of self-belief would crop up again on 2015's *To Pimp A Butterfly*.

Good Kid, M.A.A.D City (2012) was a more fully realized attempt at a concept album, an autobiographical depiction of young Kendrick growing up in Compton, an innocent corrupted by the poverty and gang culture he saw all around him. The persona presented is torn between loyalty to his family and friends, and attracted by crime, but with a growing sense of self-reflection and a yearning for escape. He collaborated with Dre on the single "The Recipe" and album track "Compton," and with Canadian superstar rapper Drake on "Poetic Justice." One of the highlights is "Sing About Me, I'm Dying of Thirst," a 12-minute epic in two parts which pays tribute to those who didn't make it out of Compton.

Lamar released his state-of-the-nation, Great American Rap Album in 2015. *To Pimp A Butterfly* dissects the ills of contemporary America and dramatizes the afflictions and complaints of the black community, in particular crime, institutional racism, and police violence. Heavily influenced by funk and jazz, it features contributions from George Clinton (see page 36), Flying Lotus, Dre, Snoop Dogg, and Ronald Isley of the Isley Brothers, and alludes to Miles Davis, James Brown, and Michael Jackson. The album cover makes explicit its political intent, showing Lamar and other black youths waving stacks of dollar bills while they occupy the White House. He explained later that the working title *To Pimp A Caterpillar* was in part a reference to Tupac (Tu P-A-C). The change to "Butterfly" shows Lamar's ambiguous feelings about society, attempting to envisage the rapacious consumption of the caterpillar as a prelude to positive change.

Lamar's lastest album, *DAMN.* (2017) is more stripped back than ...*Butterfly* but could only be considered straightforward by comparison with its predecessor. There are laid back moments, but much of *DAMN.* sounds ferocious, dense with samples, abrupt changes of rhythm, and Lamar's angry, precise, virtuosic rapping. The album concludes with a compressed short story, "DUCKWORTH.", which then dramatically cycles back to the first track. Lamar emphasised this reversible structure by later releasing a collector's edition of the album with back to front running order.

TOP ALBUM *To Pimp A Butterfly* (2015) This is a tour-de-force of jazz-inflected hip-hop that collapses the distinction between rap and performance poetry. On "For Free? (Interlude)," Lamar comes off like a manic beat poet and he teases the poem from "Mortal Man" throughout the album, adding a line each time. "King Kunta" makes explicit the connection between inequality and historical slavery by invoking the rebellious slave Kunta Kinte from *Roots*. "Alright" was adopted as the anthem of the Black Lives Matter movement. Crucially, despite its searing anger at police killings in Ferguson and elsewhere, the song's refrain, sung by omnipresent singer Pharrell Williams, chooses defiant optimism rather than despair. Elsewhere, the mood oscillates between the polar opposites of "u," a portrayal of self-hatred and doubt, and "i," which preaches a gospel of loving yourself. "i" dissolves into a capella rap in which Lamar justifies and contextualizes his frequent use of the n-word, with reference to Oprah Winfrey and Nigerian etymology. Final track, "Mortal Man," starts off as a reflection on Nelson Mandela, before segueing into the poem that Lamar has drip-fed throughout the album. Finally, he chats with his idol, Tupac, in a jazz club in heaven and relates a parable of hope that the selfish caterpillar can transform into a butterfly. Tupac does not respond.

POP TRIVIA Like Sufjan Stevens (who he sampled on "Hood Politics"), Lamar doesn't like to waste quality off-cuts. In March 2016, he released *Untitled Unmastered* via Spotify and iTunes, which consisted of eight unmastered tracks identified only by a number and date, e.g. "Untitled 01 08.19.2014." He later confirmed that they were demos or out-takes from the recording of *To Pimp A Butterfly*. A brave and thought-provoking insight into his creative process or just plain lazy? You decide.

INDEX OF ARTISTS AND TOP ALBUMS

Bold page numbers refer to main entries

★★★★ **AND FINALLY...** ★★★★★

Acknowledgments

★★★★★ ★★★★★ ★★★★★ ★★★★★

FEATURING THE FOLLOWING ARTISTS:
★★★★★ ★★★★★ ★★★★★ ★★★★★

Thanks to my wife Sally, who organized our wedding while I wrote the first edition of this book, and much love to our daughter, Jess, who deigns to dance with me in the living room to Cardiacs and Strangelove singles from the mid-1990s.

Thank you to Mum and Dad for support of all kinds, and stoking my interest in things artsy, wordy, and musical.

Thanks to Lucy Anderson and Nick Jones for making me my first mixtapes and opening my ears to the weird and wonderful world of pop music. Nick, you were right about almost all of it, but I was right about The Smiths.

A fist bump to all my fellow music geeks who I've chewed the fat with over the years, and a special FA-DA-DMP! to Adam, Emily, Rob, and Matt of one-album-wonders The Little Philistines.

Big thanks to Pete for giving me the opportunity to write and draw this book and for being so understanding when, to paraphrase Douglas Adams, the deadlines started flying by.

Thanks to Eoghan for his design prowess and Caroline for copy editing. Without them my scribbles and ramblings wouldn't seem quite so presentable.

And finally, a blanket thanks to all at BBC 6 Music, who have introduced me to so many great bands and musicians, all blissfully advert-free.

★★★★★ ★★★★★ ★★★★★ ★★★★★